Acknowledgements

Hundreds of teachers and thousands of children have participated in the National Writing Project. They have been supported by many local advisers, members of higher education colleges, parents and others in the community. We cannot name them all, but we would like to acknowledge the commitment of those participants, and trust that these publications represent at least some of their views about classroom practice.

The National Writing Project was set up by the School Curriculum Development Committee. Its three-year Development Phase (1985-1988) directly involved twenty-four local authorities and was funded jointly by the School Curriculum Development Committee and the LEAs. In 1988, the National Curriculum Council took responsibility for the Project's final implementation year.

Central Project Team (Development Phase 1985-1988)

Pam Czerniewska: Director

Eve Bearne
Barbara Grayson
John Richmond
Jeremy Tafler
} Project Officers

Naomi Baker
Anne Hogan
Judy Phillips
} Administrators

Central Project Team (Implementation Phase 1988-1989)

Jeremy Tafler: Director

Georgina Herring
Marie Stacey
} Project Officers

Rosemary Robertson: Administrator

Steering Committee

Andrew Wilkinson: Chair

Dennis Allen
Peter Andrews
Iain Ball
Douglas Barnes
Pat Barrett
Eunice Beaumont
Peter Boulter
Harold Gardiner
Alan Hall
David Halligan
John Johnson
Gulzar Kanji
Keith Kirby
Maggie Maclure
Colin Smith
June Thexton
Jenny Taylor
Mike Torbe
Janet White

Felicity Taylor: NCC Reader

Local Project Co-ordinators

Avon	Richard Bates
Bedfordshire	Mary Heath
Berkshire	Audrey Gregory
	Barry Pope
Birmingham	Ann Davis
	Sylvia Winchester
Cheshire	Gill Fox
	John Huddart
Cleveland	Margaret Meek
	Joan Sedgewicke
Croydon	Sheila Freeman
	Iain Weir
Dorset	Barbara Tilbrook
	Margaret Wallen
Dudley	Chris Morris
Durham	Dot Yoxall
Gwynedd	Len Jones
	Esyllt Maelor
	Nia Pierce Davies
Hampshire	Robin Culver
	Cath Farrow
	Ann Heslop
	Roger Mulley
Humberside	Sylvia Emerson
ILEA	Helen Savva
Manchester	Helen Henn
	Georgina Herring
Mid Glamorgan	Richard Landy
Newcastle	Jay Mawdsley
Rochdale	Frances Clarke
	Peter Phethean
	Vivienne Rowcroft
SCEA	Stuart Dyke
Sheffield	Sue Horner
Shropshire	Ned Ratcliffe
Somerset	Vernon Casey
	Maisie Foster
	Carole Mason
Staffordshire	Sallyanne Greenwood
Wiltshire	Gill Clarkson
	Sue Dean
	Jo Stone

With special thanks to Judy Phillips for her help in compiling this collection of articles.

Contents

Introduction

In 1985, the School Curriculum Development Committee set up a National Writing Project with the aim:

'. . . to develop and extend the competence and confidence of children and young adults to write for a range of purposes and a variety of audiences, in a manner that enhances their growth as individuals, their powers of self-expression, their skill as communicators and their facility as learners.'

The National Writing Project represents one of the most extensive investigations ever made into children's writing experiences in school. In 1985, at the start of the Project, a very small group of people decided to ask a very large number of teachers about their classroom practices in the teaching of writing. Those teachers' observations then served as the starting point for reflections on what might be changed, what new ideas might be introduced and how changes might best be implemented in different schools and different local authorities. The Project is, in effect, an experiment in mass consultation.

It was fortuitous that in the third year of the Project, the National Curriculum proposals took shape, national working groups were formed and the opportunity was provided for us to inform policy makers directly about conclusions reached by thousands of teachers around the country.

We made three main points to the English working group (the Cox Committee). First, we summarised teachers' observations about what writing should be like if it is to support learning. These emphasised:

- a target curriculum which provides children with purposeful writing activities for specific audiences

- a child-centred view of learning which sees children learning through experiment, building on past experiences

- activities which reflect the rich experiences of writing available in the home and the community

- tasks which recognise the complexity of the writer's behaviour from initial jottings, through many revisions, to a final outcome

- the collaborative nature of writing activities in which thoughts are written down after much discussion and texts take shape through others reading and reacting to them

- a social view of writing where writing practices are linked to cultural norms and expectations

Secondly, we argued strongly that development in writing could not be represented as a linear set of attainments. Experience of different types of writing and of different writers will lead to improved writing, but the learning process is a recursive one: children will refine their abilities each time they attempt a particular type of writing, drawing on their widening experiences.

Thirdly, we emphasised that changes, in our experience, are best made through teacher-led in-service support. We believe that the National Writing Project has been effective because teachers have been given an opportunity to articulate their own concerns, to identify particular areas for investigation, to develop activities which might lead to a more effective curriculum and to reflect on what happened in practice. This process was supported by resources which allowed discussions to take place and expertise to be shared through presentations and publications.

It was most rewarding to find that our evidence is well reflected in the National Curriculum proposals *English for Ages 5 to 11* (DES 1988). Here, emphasis is placed on the creation of a writing environment which recognises, among other things: the many purposes that writing serves; the diverse roles that teachers need to play; the need for children to experiment with writing; the task-dependence of writing competence and the recursive nature of development. The Programmes of Study for the Writing element provide guidelines for setting up a writing environment which (with some reservations) reflect the classroom practices which teachers have talked and written about in the National Writing Project publications.

Perhaps the most encouraging aspect, for us, of *English for Ages 5 to 11* is the stress placed on the provision of in-service and initial education support materials which reflect the considerable experience and expertise that already exist among teachers. (The appendices include a number of examples from the National Writing Project.)

No curriculum development project of this size is without uncertainties and tensions that sit alongside successes and agreements. After three years we had as many questions as answers about both writing and curriculum development, and the following articles bring some of these together. Each contribution is written by a co-ordinator or a central team member, and we hope that this book and the other National

Writing Project publications will enable teachers
to discuss, reflect on and promote ways of
fostering the competence and confidence of
young writers.

Pam Czerniewska

1 Looking at change — and how it happens

Reflecting on experience

Pam Czerniewska

The National Writing Project began with practice. This is not to say that it ignored theory, but those involved looked first at a complex range of classroom activities and approaches, and only later reflected on their underlying theoretical framework. I think we can identify two fundamental assumptions shared by all the thousands of participating teachers, despite their many differences in theory and practice.

The first assumption is that literacy is socially constructed; children learn to write and develop as writers in interaction with others. J.S. Bruner expresses this assumption most elegantly when he says:

'I have come increasingly to recognise that most learning in most settings is a communal activity, a sharing of the culture. It is not just that the child must make this knowledge his own, but that he must make it his own in a community of those who share his sense of belonging to a culture. It is this that leads me to emphasise not only discovery and invention but the importance of negotiating and sharing.' [1]

In the Project, children learning to be literate were not seen as pilots on solo flights, mastering a set of skills. They were perceived as learners involved in a collaborative venture.

The second assumption, which follows from the first, is that literacy is not a static concept. It is defined by a particular culture at a particular time, and that definition may be constrained by or may constrain the literacy of others. Margaret Spencer points out that, for the last hundred years or so, literacy in Western cultures has been associated with success in work, and has thus been deemed to be of general worth in the community. (This concept replaced the association of the concept of literacy with a knowledge of literature.) Work and literacy, though, are becoming less clearly related; and work is not necessarily available to all who achieve some culturally defined level of literacy. Maybe it is time for teachers, parents and politicians to broaden their view of literacy.

Children learning to read and write need to be aware of the many 'literacies' available; their uses, values and consequences

'In helping children to learn to read we, as teachers, tend to concentrate on the task in hand according to our view of it, leaving to the learners,

when they progress beyond our care, the adaptation to its functions in society of what we helped them to learn.' [2]

While these two assumptions were shared, at least implicitly, by most in the Project, their articulation was arrived at by looking at what was going on in classrooms and exchanging ideas about practice. Starting points varied, but for many an initial question was: what counts as literacy? By asking children what they thought writing was for, what makes a good/poor writer and how writers learn to write, we began to perceive how different classrooms construct literacy.

The findings are fairly well known. When asked why they write, children of all ages emphasise the importance of writing for work, for later demands. Some Durham children gave the following reasons for learning to write:

'. . . so we will know what to write in the big school . . .'

'. . . to write letters when you grow up . . .'

'. . . to write reports when you grow up . . .'

'. . . so we are ready to go in the Juniors . . .'

While there was this strong emphasis on writing and 'adultworthiness', there were also other, refreshing, reasons for writing such as that of the Newcastle five-year-old who said:

'Writing is important to us, it helps us learn. Learn to write for your own health, Mrs. Addé and God.'

As well as the prevailing association of writing with work later in life, there was an emphasis in the children's responses on neatness, correct spelling and the physical aspects of writing:

'Do you enjoy writing?'

'I don't like writing because I get flat bits at the end of my fingers.'

'Are you a good writer?'

'Bad — my spellings are wrong.'

'No — too scribbly.'

'No — I go under the lines.'

'Yes — because I use more than one piece of paper when writing stories.'

These preconceptions do not exactly reflect unwelcome views: writing *is* often useful in adult life, and it *is* often important that writing is neat and conventionally spelled so that another can understand it. What is in question is whether such a limited view of writing in school excludes children from the many other functions and values of literacy in society.

When teachers began looking at what they considered to be examples of good practice, they found that these could not be contained within one monolithic view of literacy; a view where, from the child's standpoint, writing is often initiated by teachers, and is for teachers, telling them what they already know. Writing is just too complex for that.

A few examples will illustrate the diverse functions and possible outcomes of writing. The first (below) comes from a collection of Science writing selected by teachers in Mid Glamorgan to illustrate writing for learning. Children used writing to help them observe, hypothesise, plan, test, record, evaluate and reflect. The teachers observed the significant role that 'disposable' writing — jottings, lists, rough sketches — played in the learning process.

The range of writing behaviours and the wealth of children's knowledge about writing were further demonstrated by the hundreds of children writing for audiences other than the teacher. Now, 'writing for an audience' is not a particularly new concept: all English textbooks written during this century have included sections on writing letters to someone, or writing instructions for something. The difference between these and the Project teachers' activities was that for the latter the context was real and not artificial: letters were written not (directly) to learn about letter writing, but to elicit or to acknowledge some information, and the letters were sent and replies received. Similarly, stories or guides to the school were actually read by their prospective readers. Thus the children were not solely acquiring skills to be used later; they were being writers here and now, discovering the pleasures and pains of planning what to say, researching what particular people like to read or need to know, and facing the reviews from the actual recipients of their work.

The example above — from a guide for preschoolers prepared by reception children — illustrates how even five-year-olds can be involved in decisions about appropriate information and language for younger children.

> I think that the ballon will shink because when you put a bottle top under hot water it expands so I thought that when you put the balloon under cob water it will do the oppersite

This is when we put the balloon under cold water

As soon as the emphasis of the activities changes from 'skill acquisition in preparation for the future' and becomes 'using language to achieve specific ends', the work becomes harder to place in terms of the curriculum. All subject departments become responsible for recognising children as writers. An example from an Avon Home Economics class raises a number of interesting points. The children had been making Easter nests and decided to fill them with small chocolate eggs. Each child had a packet of Cadbury's mini-eggs, and they soon realised that the packets contained different numbers of eggs. They decided to write to Cadbury informing them of their observations. The first draft of the letter looked like this:

Dear Cadburys,

~~Cadbury~~ We are a group of five pupils in the first year at Chipping Sodbury School [are intreated] to know why there are so many different numbers of eggs in an 85 gram packet of mini eggs. * we have enclosed a in our HE class graph to show you the different ranges [.]. we would so much apresheate if you would write back to tell us how why there is so much different in the packets. [/] Yours

sinserlly
Jamie
Mark

P.S. We really enjoyed your eggs   Hint! Hint

After working on this draft as a group, electing a
neat handwriter and so on, they produced a second
draft and a graph showing their findings:

Dear Cadburys,
          We are a group of five pupils
in the 1st year at Chipping Sodbury School who
are intrested to know why there are so many
diffrent numbers of eggs in an 85g packet of
mini eggs. We are using your eggs in our HE
Lesson to decorate our choclate nests. We have
enclosed a graph to show you the diffrent
ranges in our H.E class. We would so much
apriciate if you would write back to tell us
why there is so much diffrence in the packets

          Yours
               Sincerly

Becky Sweet,   Jamie Collard, Mark JENNINGS,
Michael Shaw, Anthony Patterson.

P.S. We really enjoyed your eggs.

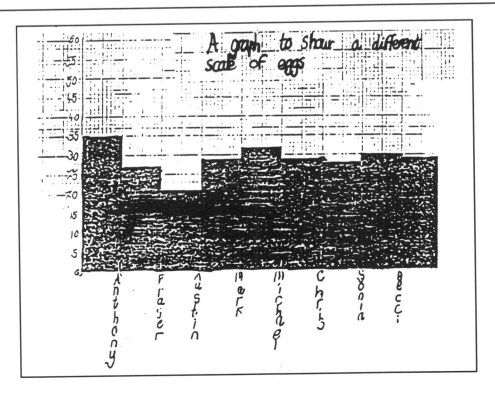

A graph to show a different scale of eggs

The final draft shows interesting amendments. There is an obvious improvement in spelling and handwriting but, more interestingly, there are features which show a recognition of the appropriate style for a friendly but complaining letter. Compare, for instance, their signatures and their postscript.

Incidentally, someone from Cadbury did reply!

These few examples demonstrate purposes, processes and products of writing that enable even the very youngest pupils to *'master meanings in new contexts, better to understand what language is and what it can do'.*[1]

The writing developed within the Project was not confined to pen and ink. Children used word processors for the planning and publishing of their work; they conveyed their messages through video, radio and other media. They learned about the constraints and the freedom of new technology.

Above all, opportunities were being created by the teacher and by the children to use language for relevant and practical purposes.

I don't think the account ends there, however. The Project has not just been 'Language in Use' revisited. We have been more radically involved in developing a view of learning which recognises the role of the learner in the construction of literacy. We have not been simply designing practical language tasks to do in class, but have been exploring the crucial interaction between child, language and task.

This interactionist perspective is witnessed most clearly in the observations of nursery and Infant teachers. What they, as other researchers, saw in samples of early writing was the wealth of literacy knowledge that young children brought to any task. Saiqa, aged five, from Manchester demonstrates how much she already knows about writing:

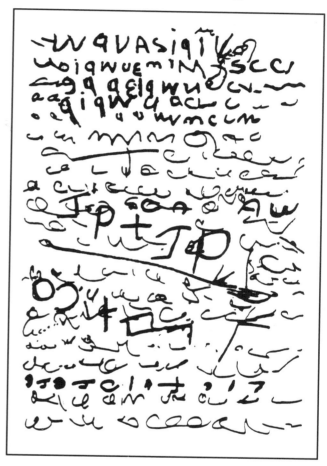

Arzoo from Cleveland shows how beginner writers are able to reconstruct the writing system so that messages can be conveyed:

I sth mumtwc

'I said to my mum it was cold'

Children not only learn from a very early age about
how writing is formed and organised, they also learn
how it is valued in their culture. A Manchester four-
year-old, for example, wrote the following:

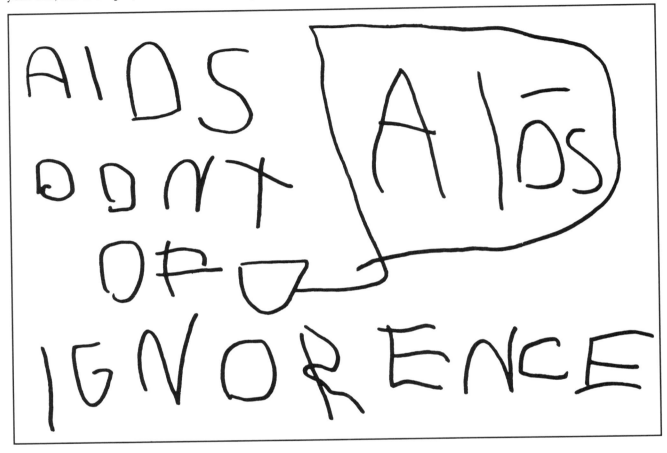

His literal memory of the AIDS poster is impressive,
as is his apparent awareness of the cultural
significance of the message.

Any examination of young children's writing reveals their urgent desire to find out how writing works and how writers behave. Steve Cummings, a nursery teacher in ILEA, experimented by putting up in the classroom, without comment, some musical notation. He watched to see what would happen, and very soon found musical notes occurring in the children's writing.

He then began talking about music and asked a Junior teacher to 'play' their writing on her guitar. Within days the children were incorporating this knowledge into their work, as one child's illustration for the story of Jack and the Beanstalk illustrates.

Children are continually making sense of the language around them; they are constructing the organisation and functions of writing on the basis of the literacy events in their world. As well as constructing language, they are constructing a way of learning and using it. An example from Lynne Carre's classroom in Devon demonstrates the role that children can have in shaping their own literacy culture. The Juniors had been looking at 'minibeasts', including a study of caterpillars. Among their supporting reading materials was Eric Carle's *The Very Hungry Caterpillar*. They decided to compare Carle's fictional account with their own observations and found a few significant discrepancies. They decided to write to Eric Carle.

Donna and Julie wrote:

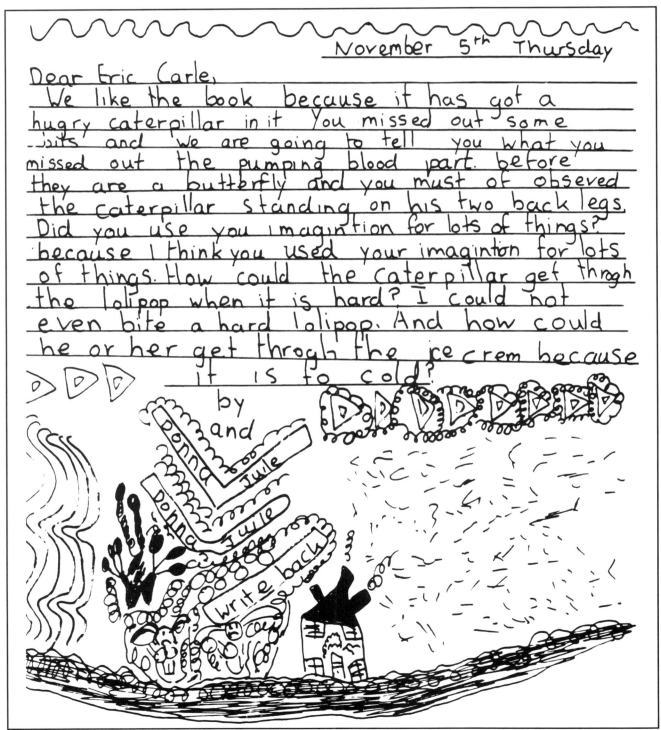

November 5th Thursday

Dear Eric Carle,
We like the book because it has got a hugry caterpillar in it You missed out some 'bits' and we are going to tell you what you missed out the pumping blood part before they are a butterfly and you must of obseved the caterpillar standing on his two back legs. Did you use you imaginition for lots of things? because I think you used your imaginiton for lots of things. How could the caterpillar get thrngh the lolipop when it is hard? I could not even bite a hard lolipop. And how could he or her get throgh the ice crem because it is to cold?

by Donna and Julie

write back

What is particularly interesting about this letter is the role these children believe they have in questioning the relationship between fact and fiction. They are actively involved in negotiating their literacy culture.

Once this type of collaboration is recognised as important in education, something happens spontaneously: the location shifts. The issue of literacy moves outside the school and involves interaction with parents, with children in other schools, with published authors, and with the local community. Project teachers have developed a writing environment for their children which engages them in, for example, publishing a community newspaper written by parents, children, teachers and others; compiling historical accounts of the community based on interviews and written anecdotes from local senior citizens; and writing with adults to produce storybooks for younger children.

The role of the teacher also changes. No longer can the success of a text be judged by the teacher alone; now there are actual consumers to evaluate its effectiveness.

Another important shift happened, too, as the multiplicity of writing practices emerged around the country. This shift was in our thinking about development. When children as young as six were writing biographical notes for the back covers of their books . . .

. . . with every child in Vivienne Miller's Dorset classroom using the third person without prompting, it became increasingly hard to talk about development as a series of stages. Young children, if given the opportunities, are able to do what older writers can do. Development needs to be seen as recursive and not linear, with children visiting and revisiting writing tasks, each time developing their understanding of the task. This view seems to be confirmed by the difficulties Government working parties have had in differentiating the National Curriculum attainment objectives for various age groups.

Overall, the Project adds up to a major reflection or rethink about:

- how we view writing: what it is for; what it is about

- how we view learners; their development and their role within the learning process

- how we organise the learning context so that it provides a range of literacy processes and products, and so that children have greater control over their learning

- how curriculum change is best achieved

It takes courage to mount a critique of a curriculum area as large as writing. It was successful because it was based on actual classroom practice, and because the teachers involved could support each other through their explorations and reflections. The pressure to change current practices came from within the classrooms — and with it came an enormous amount of hard work from the teachers, the local co-ordinators and the central team.

Thanks are due to all of these, as they are due to the children whose writing achievements continue to challenge our thinking.

References

[1] J.S. Bruner: *Actual Minds, Possible Worlds* (Harvard Educational Press 1986)

[2] M.Spencer: 'Emergent literacies: a site for analysis' from *Language Arts Vol 65(5)* (1986)

Not just in theory

Eve Bearne

When I started working with the National Writing Project there were times when I was challenged with questions which I found hard to answer. From a university lecturer: *'What is the Project's theory of writing development?'* and from a teacher: *'What do you want me to do?'* Underlying both questions were assumptions about curriculum development which reflected common experiences of previous large-scale initiatives: that curriculum development starts with a few enlightened people who explain to others a better way of teaching; and that by following a particular programme of work, or by using special materials, classroom practice will improve.

My difficulty in answering the questions was that the National Writing Project wasn't quite like that. I found myself saying, as I did so many times afterwards, *'Well, it depends . . .'* Just what it depended on was open to debate, but it wasn't a single theory about writing development.

The Project started with two interrelated intentions: to investigate writing development, and to establish effective ways of developing the curriculum. Of course there were theories. Everyone involved in the initial stages of the Project, at both national and local level, held explicit and implicit views about children, writing and classrooms. But this wasn't the point — or even the starting point. It was not with theory in its traditional sense that the teachers involved with the Project began.

They didn't start by studying what psychologists, linguists, sociologists, educationalists or other 'experts' had to say. Nor did they start by planning careful statistical sampling and predetermined investigation. They started with the implicit theories which they held about their own classrooms, those underlying ideas which prompted them to ask questions about writing. In the early stages of each local project's activities, teachers were encouraged to begin the process of examining these implicit theories and to establish principles based on their own practice. This was supported by the circulating of the national newsletter 'About Writing' and also by talks from advisers, members of the National Project's central team and other speakers who took part in launch sessions in local areas. They began the process which John Richmond has described as *'becoming our own experts'*.

This may sound simplistic (it has been criticised as *'vague'*) and was at first quite difficult to explain, both to the academic challengers and to teachers who were unsure about how they might best set about classroom investigations. Both the simplicity and the difficulty arose from a view of curriculum development which was fundamental to the shaping of the Project.

This view required a simultaneous 'unlearning' of previous methods intended to change classroom practice and an act of faith that, in the long run, a project based on teachers investigating their own concerns would, in fact, work. The teacher who asked *'What do you want me to do?'* was expressing the difficulty inherent in adopting a new way of looking at curriculum development. The question suggests that for teachers there has always been an 'expert' who could tell them what they have been doing wrong and how they might get it right, rather like a doctor who diagnoses a disease and prescribes a cure. Advisers, co-ordinators and Project Officers now had to explain that the National Writing Project was offering a framework for investigations rather than outlining the 'right' way to go about changing classroom practice. This was not about 'doing things to teachers'; it was about 'teachers doing things'. Given a structure of support at both local and national level the teachers who became involved should be able to ask — and begin to answer — their own questions. This intention was realised beyond all our expectations — although the end of the development phase left plenty of questions unresolved.

Because of this emphasis on a teacher-led initiative, the course of the Project has not been a tidy progress through clearly marked stages; it has been exploratory, wide-ranging and recursive. These elements contributed to the energy and momentum of the teachers' work but also led to some tensions. These 'healthy tensions' are inevitable in any collaborative activity, and demonstrate the fine balance between challenge and support which needs to be struck if genuine curriculum development is to take place. One of the tensions lay in the fact that the initial planning of the Project and its main areas of investigation had to be outlined before the teachers became involved. Another tension lay in the selection of participating local authorities. A restricted budget meant a limit on the number of local projects, so that selection had to be made on criteria such as geographical spread. Inevitably , this led to disappointment for some enthusiastic and supportive advisers and teachers. One attempt to maintain links between those who were interested in looking at writing in their own classrooms or institutions, but who could not be formally involved, was the establishment of a database Writing Network Directory.

Every local project had its own theme — identified by the adviser as one which might answer local needs and at the same time fit the School Curriculum Development Committee brief. The routes through which teachers became involved and the numbers of participants in local projects varied. Most were volunteers, though not all. As work progressed in local areas more teachers joined in and some dropped out. In some cases the teachers kept within the original theme; in others they pursued areas which hadn't been anticipated. Variety abounded. And yet, running throughout the work were similar threads. Whether teachers were from nursery, Infant, Junior or Secondary schools; from mainstream schools or special education; working on Maths, micros, music or any other curriculum area; whether the local project involved the community, parents or employers or looked more closely at the process of classroom writing, common factors emerged.

For example, all the teachers were very keen, right from the start, to meet and discuss the work. Even in local authorities where funding for release was very slim, teachers met, often in their own time, to exchange ideas and experiences, to describe their own work and begin to reach shared understandings. These meetings often involved colleagues from different phases and types of school and these exchanges became an important element of local investigations. Where authorities were able to fund residential meetings, collaboration developed even more quickly. Teachers who felt isolated in their own schools drew energy from talking with others who shared their concerns and aims or who had tackled the same problems. For others, the value of collaboration meant a sometimes uncomfortable shift in their thinking; but the sense that others were following similar paths meant that they could be honest about the process. As one teacher put it: *'I feel less certain about things now, and I'm pleased about that.'*

This is not to suggest, however, that simply talking with colleagues, stimulating and supportive though that may be, is enough to change classroom practice. Such meetings and discussions need a structure which will stimulate and challenge.

The importance of this kind of framework emerged as another common feature of Project work. As Michael Fullan [1] suggests, successful and continuing curriculum change emerges from a balance between pressure and support. Pressure may come from teachers who feel the need to extend or develop their practice, or who feel nagging dissatisfaction about their pupils' progress. It may come from external demands for change — from the school, the local authority or the Government. The possibility of linking with a national project gave some teachers a focus for exploring ways of dealing with their sense that there was a need for change. For others, the pressure built up slowly as they began to look more closely at their own classrooms and approaches to writing. For a small number (mainly those who were not volunteers) the pressure exerted by head teachers or the local authority proved too great a threat, and even a high level of support from local co-ordinators failed to give them sufficient confidence to question their own practices. Where the balance was right, the support needed to make pressure a positive rather than a negative force came largely from the planning and structure offered by the local co-ordinators. They listened attentively to

what teachers were saying, worked alongside them in classrooms, gave advice — but equally importantly, they provided a central point of reference for the teachers involved locally. Some co-ordinators were engaged in higher degree courses; all felt the need to think hard and long about the principles which might inform a broad and balanced writing curriculum. By organising workshop sessions, day conferences and residential meetings to tackle issues which were relevant to the local project theme or which had been identified as they emerged from the teachers' work, they created a framework through which teachers felt they could safely challenge their own thinking and that of others. At one meeting, teachers described these opportunities to share ideas as a means of *'taking the curriculum by the scruff of the neck'* and *'sharing ideas and sparking each other off'*. The contributing co-ordinators proved an important catalyst for a careful examination of classroom practice.

The framework of support was extended to offer further challenges, as teachers were encouraged to write about their work. These accounts, published locally and nationally, gave greater impetus to the teachers' investigations. The act of writing about classroom activities prompted reflection about the principles which were emerging from the work, helped to clarify thoughts and prompted further investigations. The publication of their ideas demonstrated the importance and value of the work and stimulated more teachers to take a new look at their classrooms.

The national framework also contributed some of the pressure. As part of the planned process of dissemination, local projects were asked to organise regional events where project teachers could present their work to others who had not been involved. This was indeed a challenge, since many had little experience of 'going public'. It has not been part of traditional practice for teachers' work to be valued in this way, and many felt unsure and shy. Apart from this there was the worry that no one else would be interested anyway. Who would give up their time to come and hear such classroom accounts? Thousands did. As the different events were mounted throughout England and Wales, the level of interest was encouraging and the effect was to shift the whole process up another notch from existing practice. The cycle began again. Other teachers started to identify questions about classroom writing which they wanted to pursue. After a period of observing their own practice and making explicit the areas they wanted to investigate they, too, began to talk and write about their experiences and reshape their approaches.

Those who had already been involved moved on to look more closely at the principles which were emerging from their work. They gained confidence in talking with parents and others about what they felt was important about writing. They were keen to ensure that they continued asking questions and that they should not give the impression of 'knowing how to do it'. As one teacher explained: *'We need to disseminate the approach, not the content. We must be careful not to disseminate insecurity; to add, not take away from people's confidence.'*

Continuing exploration, collaboration and partnership have been some of the common threads emerging from widely varying local projects. But perhaps the most important feature of teachers' work has been, as one of them put it, *'teachers discovering what they can do'*. The traditional 'medical' approach to in-service work, the pervasive value placed on the quiet classroom, the low status recently afforded to teachers in public debate, have led to a general sense of modesty about classroom practice. The university lecturer's question about theory becomes relevant here. For many years, teachers have been operating according to theories — mostly implicit — about children, language, classrooms and learning. The successful teacher has often diffidently dismissed a fully theorised approach to, for instance, valuing children's own language resources, as *'what I always do'*; or has seen a carefully planned series of interventions as *'just intuition'*. What has emerged from teachers' investigation — into their own classrooms and into what others have said about writing — is the recognition that theory and practice are closely intertwined. One advisory teacher who had attended a series of workshop sessions commented that she had read all the books before, but only now realised just what they were saying. For many teachers the recognition of effective new ways of working spurred them on to read more and to inform themselves about what others were saying. When reading, attending conferences or listening to visiting speakers, they were able to identify the ways in which their classroom investigations were, in fact, demonstrating theories in practice. By standing back and recognising those factors which help to promote learning, teachers have clarified the principles which inform their practice. As Bruner puts it:

'Much of the process of education consists of being able to distance oneself in some way from what one knows by being able to reflect on one's knowledge.' [2]

The teachers' reflections on their own practice led to a recognition of the importance of skilled and thoughtful organisation and intervention based on an underlying set of assumptions about language, children and learning.

In many local projects the end of the development phase was marked by meetings to summarise just what had been achieved. Another set of common experiences emerged. The words may vary, but

throughout England and Wales similar views have been voiced. These emphasise the importance of:

- recognising the learner's existing experience and building on it

- creating an environment where learners can take an active part in negotiating and organising their own learning

- providing opportunities for collaboration, reflection and evaluation

- making links and forging partnerships between all those who are involved in education

- offering challenges which can be tackled in a supportive context

- having a clear view of (and discussing) aims, purposes and intended outcomes of activities

- seeing writing as interrelated with talk, listening and reading so that language is recognised as the central means of making sense of experience and creating new knowledge

- encouraging learners progressively to take charge of their own learning

- seeing development as recursive, dynamic and cumulative rather than a linear progress through clearly defined stages

What is striking about these shared views is not so much that they should have emerged as a consensus across a national network, but that they describe the factors which govern teacher change as much as those which make for effective classroom practice.

Throughout the three-year development phase of the Project, teachers have been changing and extending their own practice through just these means. If learning — and so classroom change — is to take place there needs to be some purpose or motivation; some relevance in the task; opportunities for sharing ideas, exchanging opinions and making choices about areas of investigation; frameworks which will extend and challenge; advice from more experienced or practised colleagues; status given to individual experience; the chance to explain and justify beliefs and scope to experiment, revise and change. All of these depend upon an environment which will support and stimulate ideas. Those factors which make for more effective learning in classrooms hold true for teachers developing their own practice.

This is not to suggest that teachers involved in the National Writing Project have all the answers; nor that only the teachers who have been involved have developed effective new classroom practices to provide a broad and stimulating writing curriculum. When priority has to be given to establishing teachers' confidence in their own expertise there is a danger that celebrating success may look like complacency. On the other hand, once teachers begin to believe in their own ability to change the curriculum, there is a greater likelihood that they will challenge themselves. We need to assert clearly and forcefully just what has been achieved — not just for teachers, but most importantly for children, who have often surprised their teachers by showing remarkable capacities for using writing to fulfil their own intentions. The evidence of their achievements has been taken seriously by national committees: TGAT, Kingman and Cox. If teachers are to use the introduction of the National Curriculum to continue and extend effective practices for encouraging a broader writing curriculum, the successes have to be kept firmly in mind.

And what of the failures, or perhaps more accurately, the gaps in the achievements of the National Writing Project? There are several. Since a curriculum development initiative based on teachers identifying their own concerns will necessarily be a long-term process of change, several important issues still remain to be tackled: questions of gender and culture; ways in which teachers can help children identify the forms of writing required by different genres and develop critical readership. Although a great deal has been achieved in understanding and fostering early literacy, the Secondary sector has remained relatively untouched.

Perhaps in the future we shall be able to judge just how effective teacher-led initiatives can be. If the new ways of working have taken root, these gaps will be filled. If local authorities can acknowledge the value of supporting teachers with advisory staff and time, it is more likely that the difficult issues can be tackled. In many Project areas, co-ordinators have become members of advisory teams and the model of curriculum development has become institutionalised in some way. This validates the importance of starting from practice in order to articulate theory. It gives status to teachers' work and recognises the value of starting in the classroom.

From teachers' implicit theories which have informed practice, principles emerge which move towards explicit theory: about language and learning as active, dynamic and interrelated; about writing as a unique means of generating ideas, clarifying and crystallising thought and communicating intentions effectively; about classrooms as environments which will recognise and stimulate children's own language and provide experiences which will help them to increase their facility in written expression. The traditional view of children as passive receivers of knowledge becomes supplanted by the evidence from classroom investigations into children's language resources and their active creation of knowledge through writing. Recognising that learning is most effective and lasting when it is the result of active participation means that learning 'how to' becomes as important as learning 'what'.

Those teachers who have worked on local projects, and many others, have demonstrated that reflection on both process and content — 'how to' as well as 'what' — is necessary for a fully theorised approach to learning. As one teacher explained: *'I used to be a teacher of History; now I say that I am a teacher of language and History'.*

This greater understanding of how learning happens — a *'new way of working'* as another teacher described it — best expresses the relationship between theory and practice. Neither is more important than the other, nor does one take place before the other; they are interdependent elements in effective learning. Wherever that learning takes place, in the classroom or amongst a group of teachers, those factors which make for recognition of that interrelatedness will ensure future learning. It's not only *'I know that'* but also *'I know what I can do with that'* which makes the difference. Nobody involved in the National Writing Project would claim to have found all the answers. What has been established is a way of continuing to tackle the questions.

References

[1] M. Fullan: *The Meaning of Educational Change* (Teachers' College Press, Columbia University 1982)

[2] J.S. Bruner: *Actual Minds, Possible Worlds* (Harvard Educational Press 1986)

Rewriting the syllabus

Richard Landy

Looking back on it all, I can see where I went wrong. As head of an English department in a typical Secondary school, I dutifully spent six years, off and on, talking to colleagues (or, more probably, at them) about the urgent need for a school policy for language across the curriculum. I addressed meetings. I wrote documents. I manoeuvred subtly and I made outright demands. I argued, confronted and sulked. I don't think it got me very far. There were some simple truths about curriculum development which I hadn't learned. Perhaps I still tended to consider policy in an abstract rather than a practical sense? As teachers, we have a healthy distrust of sterile documentation, but we do enjoy doing things together, particularly when they work. It's practice that makes policy, not paper.

Some eighteen months into the Writing Project, my diary contained the following entries relating to Project activities at one Secondary school in Mid Glamorgan:

'2nd March: World of Work group: joint meeting with local employers

4th March: Visit by Liz V. from Hampshire

11th March: Pupils collating material for "Caerphilly Campaign" special issue

14th March: Llanbradach bypass project group meeting

22nd March: World of Work group: planning response to employers

24th March: Meeting Olwyn H. and pupils at "Campaign" offices

28th March: Llanbradach bypass: presentation to other pupils

29th March: Planning meeting for years 1/2 "Our School" project

30th March: "Home Front" presentation for senior citizens'

Now here's a writing policy in action! It's worth considering how and why all this activity — involving teachers from almost all curriculum areas and pupils of all ages — came about.

Working groups can be difficult. I can remember the first meeting of our group quite vividly. It was a very tentative occasion. Olwyn, who had recently been given responsibility for language across the curriculum, had convened the group by asking for volunteers, twisting a few arms in the process. All of us were willing but unsure of each other and, perhaps, ourselves. We broke the ice by talking about the kinds of writing demands we made of pupils in our different subject areas, taking, as a starting point, a list of very straightforward but fundamental questions, such as: *'Who are they writing for?' 'Where are they writing?' 'What do we do with what they've written?'*

On looking back at the notes of that meeting, it's interesting to see the general conclusions which we reached. We commented that much of the pupils' writing was done with the intention (our intention, that is!) of collating information into a usable form which would itself become a learning resource. We noted that our pupils often seemed to perceive writing as a necessary proof that learning had taken place. Invariably, we felt, our pupils were asked to write in an impersonal way. (One of us commented that he always told his pupils to *'leave out the "I"'.*) We conceded that, generally, our pupils were given little opportunity to work on their writing for more than a very brief period of time, that the vast majority of tasks were one-off writing assignments, and that the idea of reworking writing through a process was one which, for a variety of reasons, was largely ignored. When we came to discuss what we actually did with the writing our pupils undertook for us, we all admitted to assessment, but very little else. We talked about the reasons for all this: the constraints under which we felt we operated in our different subject areas and the pressures of time caused by syllabus content and requirements.

Aware of the dangers of generalisation, we agreed to begin our investigation by trying to obtain some sort of snapshot of our pupils' writing diet, first by looking at some examples of written work that pupils had recently done, and secondly, by persuading two classes of pupils to keep writing diaries in which they recorded: what they wrote, the nature of the task, the amount of writing done, the time available, the audience and any further comments they wished to add.

The diaries, rough and ready blunt instruments that they were, turned out to be a good place to start — particularly in a Secondary school where, of course, there is a real danger that nobody is taking an overall view of the writing that pupils are asked to undertake during the course of a day, a week or a year. Those dividing walls of the Secondary curriculum can be very high and rigid at times. When we peered over, I think we were all genuinely surprised, even in the light of our earlier comments, by: the sheer quantity of 'end product' writing pupils were expected to produce, the limited opportunities available for redrafting or editing, the lack of choice of task or format, and the 'teacher-centredness' of an activity for which the teacher was, invariably, the only audience. It was a picture which didn't seem to vary much from subject to subject. In a way it deflated us, but at least the diaries had identified some aspects of writing which clearly needed further investigation and development.

Looking at each other's examples was much more difficult. In retrospect, perhaps this was the wrong time to do this. Even though the members of the group knew each other very well, because we were all from different subject areas we weren't necessarily used to working with each other. We hadn't had the time to develop, for example, a shared vocabulary, and we didn't yet have that sense of collective enterprise which is so necessary for groups such as this. Consequently, we were all very wary of asking each other the very basic questions that we needed to ask about pupils' work. We remained polite. Trust takes time to establish. Good friends in the Secondary staffroom can remain very distant professionally!

Meanwhile, I was quietly beginning to panic. Where on earth were we going? How were we going to get our investigations started while everybody was being so very careful about what they shared and said? Who was going to take the plunge?

Ed did. Ed is head of the Geography department. In our first discussions about the writing demands made of pupils in our different subjects, Ed had talked about what he saw as the difficulty of reconciling a more open approach to writing with his concerns for subject content and methodology. He said that he'd considered trying out such approaches in the past but had always ended up asking himself, *'But is it really Geography?'* Unbeknown to the rest of the group, Ed decided to see for himself what might happen when a more open approach to writing tasks was adopted. He experimented by encouraging a class of first year pupils to write freely about a set of contrasting landscapes/cityscapes. Surprised not only by the empathetic quality of their writing but also by their willingness to speculate about what was shown in the pictures, he decided to extend his investigation by inviting groups of fifth year pupils to write, in role, as various interested parties in an inquiry concerning the proposed closure of a local colliery. Finding that such an approach could produce writing that most certainly was Geography, and effective Geography at that, Ed came to our next meeting with examples of the pupils' work to show us.

That first investigative work of Ed's was the crucial moment in our group's development. Until that point we'd been on safe if unfamiliar ground, in that we were still just talking rather than doing. The fact that Ed was prepared to try something different in his classroom and return to share what had happened with a group of 'curricular strangers' made, I think, all the difference. His example certainly encouraged us to begin to undertake classroom work ourselves. A series of after-school meetings followed during the next few months, as members of the group took it in turn to describe and show to the rest of us what they'd been doing to investigate those issues about writing which our first discussions and then our diary-survey had raised. Different members of the group took up different issues in different ways. In Maths, John investigated

ways of helping his pupils in the reporting of their investigative work for GCSE. In French, Olwyn's pupils worked in groups to make information sheets for other, younger pupils. Cory experimented by allowing her RE pupils to determine their own mode and format for reporting their discussions. Fay looked at ways of using writing to foster empathy in her History pupils. Alan's less confident pupils discovered the potential of the microcomputer to help with the writing and production of storybooks for younger pupils.

I sometimes wondered whether this was really the right approach. Shouldn't we be tackling one issue at a time — and tackling it as a group? Was there a danger of the work losing its coherence and sense of direction? With hindsight, I think that in the case of our group we were probably right to proceed in the way we did. Dealing with all the issues one at a time would not have been a realistic option for a group which was meeting voluntarily, out of school hours. The way in which we worked also allowed different members of the group to identify their own priorities for investigation — necessary in a group containing teachers from such a wide range of curriculum backgrounds. The variety also helped us to keep our momentum. Often, one teacher's activity sparked off another's, and we found ourselves continually asking new questions and identifying further issues.

The synthesis began to emerge with time. It became clearer and clearer that most of our subject-based concerns with writing were, in fact, shared concerns about the role of writing in learning. When Fay observed that Cory's pupils' reports of their findings on the subject of prejudice had a direct relevance to the work her pupils were doing on the rise of Fascism, it sparked off the idea of tackling the writing issues we wanted to investigate through a genuinely cross-curricular collaboration. For all of us, this seemed a logical extension of the work we'd been developing in the Project so far. However, agreeing on a topic or theme for collaboration was a more difficult matter. Experience with another working group in a Secondary school where some of the teachers had decided to work together in this way had suggested to me that, in a cross-curricular project, it's quite important to try to move away from the usual syllabus content. One of the difficulties that the other group had experienced in an otherwise successful investigation was that, for all sorts of reasons, teachers sometimes tend to come to familiar material with a predetermined approach. We tried to build on that group's experience by choosing topics for our investigations which would involve new content for the classes concerned. Eventually, we settled on a subdivision of our (now extended!) working group into two parallel groups, both concerned with the planning of a programme of work which would cross curricular boundaries and, we hoped, generate a more open and balanced diet of writing for the pupils concerned. One group worked on a programme for a specific third year class on the theme of 'The Home Front' in English, French, History, Home Economics and RE. The other group, involving teachers of English, Geography, Maths and Science, brought a variety of fourth year classes into collaboration on the topic of plans for a local bypass. Both groups planned to work to a tight schedule, involving pupils in roughly six weeks' work. In the event, the collaboration took months rather than weeks, as the pupils' work developed in ways which the groups hadn't anticipated. A major learning outcome for the teachers concerned was the need to plan such collaborative enterprises on a more flexible basis. It takes only an unforeseen spin-off or a staff absence for the best laid plans to go awry! In the case of the 'Home Front' work this occurred when the third year class decided that the most appropriate way for them to communicate the learning that had taken place would be to stage a massive end-of-term presentation for other pupils and parents, involving a range of displays and activities including an hour-long musical production written and performed by the pupils. One teacher from outside the group commented that their presentation demonstrated more learning than several exercise books full of notes ever could.

The group working on the theme of the local bypass demonstrated that GCSE coursework requirements in different subject areas could be satisfied more coherently for the pupils through cross-curricular collaboration. For example, a survey of local residents' feelings was designed during English lessons, went through a process of data analysis and graphical representation in Maths, and found its way into pupils' Geography folders as part of their GCSE submission on the topic. At this level, cross-curricular collaboration can not only expand and broaden the writing diet, but also rationalise the sometimes burdensome demands which are made of pupils.

As the extracts from my diary for March demonstrate, development has continued. Further cross-curricular programmes, gradually involving more and more members of staff, have evolved from that initial work. First and second year pupils have been working with teachers from different subject

areas on the production of an information pack about 'Our School' for next year's intake. Pupils in the fifth and sixth years have been making their own newspaper about the world of work. Discussions about writing inside and outside school have been broadened through the involvement of ex-pupils and employers. As I said at the beginning of this article, this seems to me to be the best kind of writing (or language) policy — one which is driven by the notion of teachers working at shared concerns by investigating them together.

Of course, this isn't the only possible approach to that vexed question of how to get at the writing and learning issue with colleagues from different curriculum areas. Where it's possible to bring teachers of, for example, Maths or Science together to look at the role of writing in learning in a particular area of the curriculum, much can be achieved. However, within the context of a typical Secondary school, such as the one referred to here, there exists additional potential for collective investigation — a resource too rich to be ignored.

What conclusions might be drawn from our experience in Mid Glamorgan, as typified by the case of this particular school? I would identify four major ones. The first is that the development of a school writing policy should not be English-led. In the school in question, the English department was certainly involved, but, sensibly, never attempted to dominate discussion or determine direction. If it is to be successful in practice, a writing policy needs to be commonly owned.

The second conclusion is that the best way of developing a policy is through a programme of practical investigation, rather than through planning on paper.

The third is that in the context of a Secondary school, cross-curricular collaboration is a very effective way of bringing shared concerns about writing and learning into the open, and of generating the necessary dynamic for change.

The fourth and final conclusion is inescapable. It is that if genuine development is to occur, it is vital that provision is made for teachers from different curriculum backgrounds to meet, talk and reflect together, and that those teachers are supported effectively in their enterprise.

Instruments of change

Jay Mawdsley

'They were nothing more than people, by themselves. Even paired, in any pairing, they would have been nothing more than the people by themselves. But all together, they have become the heart and muscles and mind of something perilous and new, something strange and growing and great.

'Together — all together, they are the instruments of change.' [1]

Each of the twenty-four local education authorities within the National Writing Project had its own appointed project co-ordinator and, with organisation of the individual projects directly affected by local demands and finances, the support offered to teachers and co-ordinators varied considerably. Although this diversity of experience must underpin any general consideration of the project co-ordinator's role, I offer my own experience and observations from the viewpoint of the reflective practitioner, attempting to resolve some of the ambiguities and complexities of the relationship between effort and effect in supporting curriculum change and development. Each co-ordinator will recall different high and low points: key elements that seemed to be successful in their own particular context, and, conversely, those moments of frustration or isolation common to all projects. This paper seeks to draw out from the particular some thoughts on the support system that might best serve the co-ordinators, the support teachers, of curriculum development projects.

The nature of the role of 'curriculum support' or 'advisory' teachers affects and is affected by both national and local requirements. The apparently well defined role of 'curriculum support teacher' belies the multi-faceted reality. However, once curriculum support is seen to involve development, which by definition involves change, the delicate nature of the task is revealed. As agents of this process of change, co-ordinators are charged with adopting a Janus-like role: encouraging and supporting teachers whilst asking them at the same time to examine their own practice. From the outset of a curriculum development project, they should be aware that it is in the nature of change to cause imbalance and frequently a period of ensuing discomfort; curriculum development is concerned with challenging existing convictions and existing practice, and co-ordinators must be concerned with providing both the challenge and the support to effect these changes. It is a paradoxical role, and there are occasions when the hollow laughter of overworked classroom teachers echo in one's ears. Michael Fullan's assessment of the dilemmas of engendering change may help to provide a balanced view of the 'change process' equation:

'The fact that those who advocate and develop change get more rewards than costs, and those who are expected to implement it experience many more costs than rewards, goes a long way in explaining why the more things change the more they remain the same.' [2]

If the major task of a project co-ordinator is to support change, it may be worthwhile taking time in the early stages of a project to address some of the following issues:

- how best to offer support whilst simultaneously encouraging change

- how to raise issues without dismantling confidence

- how to offer advice whilst enabling people to discover and learn from their own experience

- how to recognise that time is not elastic and that most teachers have a wide variety of school commitments

- how to develop the skills of attentive listening and close observation whilst retaining objectivity

- how to build existing skills into the process of change

- how to help people realise their personal goals without losing sight of the project context

- how to establish a clear commitment between schools and the project

- how to recognise that a co-ordinator's time is not infinite; how to say no

Neat resolutions to these questions may not be immediately forthcoming; in fact there may be ambiguities that merit a co-ordinator's sensitive consideration.

Throughout the duration of the Writing Project, the paramount responsibility of all co-ordinators was the support of classroom teachers within their local project — teachers who, together, have formed a vast national network of curriculum development. Without these teachers there would be no Writing Project, and yet initially the Project's central team offered teachers no single panacea towards resolving concerns they had already identified about their pupils' written work.

Within the broad structure and organisation of curriculum development projects, powerful messages are relayed to the participants: too many directives or too much domination by research institutes may militate against genuine partnership. The Project brief signposted democratic intent by proposing a National Writing Project for children and young adults '. . . *(to enhance) their growth as individuals, their powers of self-expression, their skill as communicators and their facility as learners'.* By avoiding the imposition of a centralised model, the SCDC steering group provided a context for the formulation of devolved project bids, leaving the exact nature of the model to be defined by each participating LEA.

26

It is fair to say that, at first, teachers within the Newcastle project were not wholeheartedly enthusiastic about the implications of the devolved, partnership model of curriculum development adopted at a local level. Some teachers thought that their needs and those of the Project would be better served by a series of clear guidelines in the form of reading lists, whilst others would have welcomed staged guidelines towards independent writing in the classroom. The process of change might well have been accelerated by both these means, but superficial, prescriptive measures would have undermined the Project's belief in basing curriculum development upon the experience of the classroom practitioner.

This initial period of uncertainty provided a hiatus during which teachers began raising questions for themselves as they gradually assumed the role of classroom researcher: observing, hypothesising, trialling, reflecting — and emerging with a new synthesis of understanding. When, towards the end of the first year of the Project, Newcastle teachers were asked to reflect on their initial insecurity, many recognised this as an early stage in the development of their approach to writing. For a project co-ordinator, the temptation to offer support by sweeping in with myriads of ideas and suggestions in order to 'get the show on the road' should be resisted. Like good classroom teachers, they are there as facilitators — not providers of a package.

Support for the co-ordinator in reconciling local and national concerns comes from a variety of sources; in the case of the National Writing Project, the designated central team officer, the LEA subject adviser, and a network of fellow co-ordinators. The central team of a project, with an overview of national patterns of curriculum development, may at times set expectations that seem in danger of jeopardising carefully fostered relationships between local co-ordinators and project teachers, and it is then that conflicts of intent may emerge. The launch of regional events, to disseminate more widely the developments of the Writing Project, was an example of this during the second term of our involvement.

The timing of the request for a regional event seemed to deny the process model of curriculum development promoted by the Project; at a relatively early stage, were we not being asked to produce a product for display? As co-ordinator, my goal for the first year was to allow time for the Newcastle teachers to consolidate their own thinking and development before taking on the pressures of presenting workshops for teachers outside the Project; teachers who might well be looking for the proverbial 'tips for teachers'. However, I was persuaded by the project officer that the relatively small number of participating

LEAs demanded a concerted national effort in the dissemination of new developments. My role was now to develop a strategy that would give teachers the confidence to undertake such an event. The project officer, fellow co-ordinators and I devised a schedule of workshops — on running workshops — for all project teachers in the north-east, and the regional event for two hundred and fifty teachers took place. Yes, the teachers and co-ordinators were anxious, but the knowledge that their experience was valued in a wider educational forum gave the project teachers an immediate sense of euphoria, and the subsequent motivation and confidence to continue providing INSET courses on varying aspects of early writing. Although my initial concerns about the event were justified in a local context, on reflection I felt that the external stimulus and support had helped to foster the self-confidence of the project teachers. The experience of organising and running a regional event formed an important basis for the second year of the Newcastle project; taking part in a well publicised public event had demonstrated, far more eloquently than I could have done, that Newcastle was part of a major curriculum development project that valued the classroom teacher.

In my initial ambivalence about the regional event, I recognised certain parallels with the way in which some of my suggestions were received by project teachers. They too were dealing with conflicting demands — some coming from within school — of which I was often unaware. Without absolving co-ordinators of the responsibility for guiding a project, I feel that teachers, like co-ordinators, benefit from the opportunity to draw on the support found in a network of colleagues involved with similar daily pressures and willing to share in the planning and evaluation of classroom-based curriculum development. Newcastle's project model provided an additional layer of support within the larger context of the city: small cluster groups of teachers from four project schools. The three cluster leaders — who had been allowed two and-a-half days each week to participate — supported teachers with their classrooms and formed an informal research group, meeting regularly to discuss and evaluate progress with the co-ordinator.

Support groups for teachers also become support groups for co-ordinators as a project gathers pace, but in the early stages the meetings of these groups are often extremely tentative; much depends on the individuals. The Newcastle project reflected a belief that the selection of schools will have a direct influence on the long-term outcomes of curriculum change. Rather than extending an open invitation to the project, we identified particular Newcastle schools to represent the full range of catchment areas in the city; teachers in these schools were then included in the project according to the age range they were teaching. We believed that in this way, our findings would have relevance to all schools; they could not be ignored or even rejected on the grounds that curriculum change can be effected only in schools which are socially, educationally or economically advantaged. This pattern of selection involves a conundrum for the co-ordinator: the possibility of working with teachers who have no particular interest in the specific field of enquiry. Once more, one is dealing with the dynamics of control versus democracy. There is no one correct way in which to set up a project, but for a co-ordinator the initial choices will affect the nature of the project's support structure.

Within the organisational framework of a project, a co-ordinator hopes to provide a role model for curriculum development within the classroom. In practice this means demonstrating a democratic model of leadership, and being prepared to accept differing attitudes to the project. Not all teachers receive new ideas with confidence and enthusiasm; project teachers, like project co-ordinators, are a prey to their own past experiences and current uncertainties. The creation of *a collaborative spirit of enquiry*[3] should imply opportunities for risk taking as well as opportunities for a more gradual process of change. The nature of this sensitive process may best be illustrated by quoting from a letter that I received from a project teacher:

'. . . I feel I should write you a little note apart from the questionnaire. As a "pressed man" rather than a volunteer to the Writing Project I must say how grateful and pleased I am to have been involved. Yes, it is a lot of hard work (and as an initial response I will probably always moan when I am asked to write a "short account" or give up a Saturday) . . . For myself, I have found the involvement in the Project to be a most rewarding experience. English has never been my strong point and I think I have always found writing to be difficult. Perhaps in the past my classes have found Maths etc. to be more interesting and enjoyable than writing. This is certainly not true now! I have never seen children so enthusiastic about writing, choosing to go into the writing corner in preference to other activities. This must be my awareness and "confidence" rubbing off on them.

'I am sure that I have been cast as the "black sheep" in the group but honestly this is not intentional — probably more my insecurity initially — everyone seemed to know so much more about it than I did and I find it difficult to talk about the work I have done. However, I can only say that this year has been most successful if the enthusiasm of my class is anything to go by.

'Thanks again.'

This letter reinforced my belief in the importance of devolution: we make real choices and their

attendant outcomes clear and available to young children, and should adopt the same principle for teachers working on curriculum development projects. Carl Rogers puts it like this: *'The more I am open to the realities in me and in the other person, the less do I find myself wishing to rush in to "fix things".'*[4] Devolving control within education does not mean abandoning the learners and should not be construed as the easy option. Project members have the right to expect input and support from a co-ordinator, but the nature of a devolved project means that participants have responsibilities to fellow members, and are not answerable only to the nominally responsible figure of the co-ordinator. A project support system that directly involves teachers can evolve into an active and potent force for change. As teachers share their observations, concerns, evidence and delights, they move towards an unreserved dialogue, a mutually beneficial curriculum activity.

What, then, is the role of the co-ordinator; how can it be defined and by whom? Do project teachers need someone who will: raise issues rather than provide answers; produce evidence from other projects and from relevant research to set against their own classroom evidence; present opportunities for teachers to learn from each other in a variety of forums; act as a clearing house for ideas; help disseminate findings; be prepared to listen? Is this hypothetical 'co-ordinator's catechism' one that would fulfil the definition of a co-ordinator put forward by the central team, by an LEA or by project teachers? Running a project will certainly effect change for the co-ordinator; to be involved with fostering the process of change in others is to become inextricably caught up with the process of change oneself.

Perhaps the most telling support system for any co-ordinator is the network which gradually develops, crisscrossing the landscape both metaphorically and literally. From fragile beginnings, people across the country have forged a collaborative project, infused with a common intent and built upon a foundation of experiential learning meeting personally perceived needs. For teachers and project co-ordinators the most valuable and yet the most scarce commodity has been time. Surely, engagement in any serious curriculum investigation requires an extensive investment of time and energy, if the findings are to transcend the superficial.

Unfortunately, the purchase of tangible goods seems to attract a more sympathetic response from budget planners than the prospect of funding time out of the classroom for teachers — or even reimbursing teachers for enriching their understanding of a subject in meetings after school and at weekends. With an injection of time, it is possible for co-ordinators to ask more of teachers already overburdened with their regular school commitments, and it becomes feasible for classroom teachers to ask more of themselves. When there is time for reflection, investigation functions within a receptive framework; new ideas can be explored and evaluated without the erection of defensive barriers. Time provides space for people to discover that *'what is most personal is most general'*,[4] and to immerse themselves in the often messy process of change.

Time enables co-ordinators to keep abreast of national and international developments in the field, and to bring relevant findings into the local context of enquiry. Subject advisers, who most often initiate the project bids, need time to meet with their co-ordinators. They can provide invaluable advice on unfamiliar administrative procedures, and their experience provides a valuable sounding board for untried ideas. Co-ordinators need sufficient time to launch ideas, confident in the knowledge that they will still be there later to support the teachers. An LEA might offer, for example, a specific allocation of secretarial help, but ultimately all support seems to

be connected with the time factor. Projects should not be planned as neat financial packages with any continuation phase left to chance; the ultimate time resource would be sufficient funding to enable further development and dissemination on an official basis. Too often, this kind of follow-up relies on the goodwill of project teachers.

Curriculum development offers a wealth of opportunities for learning about a particular curriculum area but also, as a co-ordinator or advisory teacher, one is simultaneously concerned with learning about the management and organisation of curriculum change. One project does not make an expert, and each project will have different requirements with new challenges. Working with the National Writing Project has affirmed the importance of creating a climate of freedom for a collaborative, decentralised model of effective enquiry and curriculum change. Many people have gained by sharing their expertise, confident in the knowledge that *'Together, all together, they are the instruments of change.'*[1]

References

[1] K. Hulme: *The Bone People*
(Hodder & Stoughton 1985)

[2] M. Fullan: *The Meaning of Educational Change*
(Teachers' College Press, Columbia University 1982)

[3] L. Stenhouse: *An Introduction to Curriculum Research and Development* (Heinemann 1975)

[4] C. Rogers: *On Becoming a Person*
(Houghton Mifflin 1961)

A countywide model   Gill Clarkson, Sue Dean and Jo Stone

This is an account of the development of the Wiltshire and Somerset Write to Learn Project. It is not offered as a fixed model; its growth has been organic, and its present shape is the result of the environment in which it has developed, nurtured by the care, concern and enthusiasm of all who have become involved. Our project is firmly rooted in the belief that:

- teachers are concerned with the quality of what they offer their pupils

- they care about their own classroom practice and are interested in approaches to learning which support and help to extend it

- they are willing to take on and develop new teaching strategies

Two years ago we set out to demonstrate that our project might help children to:

- make connections between new and existing knowledge

- discover what they thought and understood

- speculate, experiment and take risks in writing

- enjoy writing what they wanted to write

- appreciate both the writing process and its products

Taking on new ideas and changing classroom practice is a risky business, and we were aware that teachers interested in change would need support from us and from each other: opportunities to exchange ideas, to share problems and successes, jointly to extend their own practice and understandings. As interest in the project grew, so the nature of the co-ordinators' task became clearer.

We needed to create opportunities to demonstrate strategies to teachers and to provide support through: working with teachers in their classrooms; liaising with colleagues, head teachers, parents and governors; creating local workshop groups for sharing and discussion, for the presentation of further strategies and the distribution of relevant literature; and, finally, disseminating our discoveries across the two counties and to other LEAs and institutions.

We began with five introductory workshops, offered countywide, during the course of a term. After a short introduction to explain our basic belief in the capacity of all children to make sense of and through writing, teachers participated in a range of writing strategies such as brainstorming, 'burst' writing, drafting, and talking together to extend or to clarify meaning.

In these introductory sessions, we ourselves wrote — 'think-writing' — and discussion focused attention on what had helped or hindered the process of shaping meaning in writing, and enabled teachers to consider the differences between what had helped them to write and the constraints so often imposed on their pupils. Writing for themselves reminded teachers that thinking is often a messy process, but the untidiness of their own brainstormed lists or scribbled first drafts did not negate the value of the content nor the potential for further shaping.

As a result of these introductory days, many teachers were keen to try new writing strategies in their own classrooms, and to meet to share their discoveries and discuss any problems. We then established area workshops, which met three or four times a term, to enable this exchange to take place.

Wiltshire and Somerset were fortunate, at the beginning of the project, to have a nucleus of teachers who had been involved in the LEA's Learning about Learning Project. These Primary, Middle and Secondary school teachers (ten each year from each county) had worked closely together in a residential institute at the start of the summer holidays, taking part in activities which led to more effective learning for their pupils and themselves. They had subsequently helped to run programmes of after-school or evening workshops for other teachers. These experienced teachers helped us to organise our initial workshops. Without their help, the co-ordinators would not have been able to initiate a countywide programme so quickly.

These area workshops have become the seedbeds out of which the project has grown. The workshops have developed differently according to the needs and demands of their members, but most have a mixed programme of activities, in which teachers present particular ideas and strategies, allowing time for discussion. In Somerset, the workshops have been led by teachers in the project; this leadership can continue when the funding ends.

Discoveries made at presentations often form a basis for the work, although of course this is not always so. Individual teachers have different starting points, different priorities and different contexts for work. It is important to respect the teachers' own autonomy and remember the constraints within which they must work; not every teacher will want, or be able, to move in step with colleagues. The sessions are also important because the group can confirm its own efforts. Looking closely, as a group, at the development of a child or a group of children helps to raise the level of critical thinking, and focuses attention in a way which is seldom possible for a teacher operating on his/her own.

The workshops have created a network of local support: teachers can plan work together, write for each other's classes, visit one another's classrooms. This network of supportive, interested teachers is especially important for those teachers working in small village schools, with only one or two colleagues, or those working in environments which do not support their efforts.

When teachers want to try new strategies, the Write to Learn Project is able to offer a range of classroom support, depending on their needs at the time. These include:

- initiating whole class activities, when the teacher is free to be a participant observer
- working with small groups within the class
- planning new starting points and activities
- offering particular skills such as book-making
- simply being there to boost confidence

Discussion always precedes and follows these sessions: considering what might meet, or has met, the needs of particular children; how the activity could be extended or developed; what other support could be offered. The co-ordinators' main concern is to work in partnership with teachers to create increasingly effective contexts for learning inside their classrooms.

Invitations to work in schools have been useful in a variety of ways:

- They enable us to show that project strategies work in practice as well as in theory.
- They highlight the work of the project, making other teachers in the schools aware of our existence.
- They give status to the work of the individual teachers.
- The work provides a starting point for informal staffroom discussion.

As a result of such visits and the teachers' enthusiasm, colleagues from their schools have now joined our workshops and become part of the project. This has resulted in a growing number of requests to organise in-service training days for a whole school, or for groups of schools. The programme for these in-service days often depends on the head teacher's perception of needs and, of course, the current level of teacher involvement in the project. Whatever the programme, we make the days as active as possible, involving committed classroom teachers if we can. As co-ordinators we are seconded out of our own classrooms and so are open to the charge that we are unaware of the real problems of initiating change in schools. If teachers can talk to others about their successes and problems, and can show real examples of work resulting from our project's approach, this has credibility and conviction. We always provide time during these days for teachers to think and talk about their own attitudes, preconceptions, doubt and confusion. Again, classroom teachers can do much to counter the argument that the changes of

emphasis we suggest are unworkable within a real classroom context. We have ample evidence to show that they are not.

Change always has to be justified, and the increasing powers given to parents and governors have made it vital for teachers to explain clearly what happens in their classrooms — and why. Increasingly, we have been asked to set up workshops to introduce and explain new initiatives within the schools, and to assure parents and governors that the Write to Learn Project does not advocate the abandonment of correct spelling, syntax, punctuation and neat presentation. In our experience, once this has been explained, parents and governors not only accept our approach but are enthusiastic about the opportunities that writing provides for their children to think and shape meaning, before they move on to corrections and proof-reading. As with all the workshops we run, participation is the key, and we try to take these adults — many of whom have been persuaded that they 'cannot write' by their own school experiences — through a range of collaborative writing strategies. Active writing helps them to focus on what is important about the writing process, and to realise that 'getting it right' is an important concern but one which can be pursued after the initial meaning making. At the end of our sessions many parents admit that, in their own workplace, thinking is valued more than dictionary or keyboard skills, and that they place much reliance on secretaries for the accuracy and appearance of the final written product!

Looking at examples of children's work, both process and product, helps them to appreciate the power to think in written words, which children of all ages show. The think-writing, the drafting and the redrafting make them aware of the hard work which lies behind the production of a short poem, a simple story or a problem-solving exercise. Too often we show parents only the finished product, leaving them unaware of the thought and effort which have gone into it.

A teacher's job is hard: the curriculum has to be covered, and thirty or more inquisitive, developing minds have to be stretched and involved. It is important, then, to provide opportunities for teachers to consider their own practice, and develop their own writing freed from professional demands. In our joint project, we provide such opportunities through residential weekends which we offer to involved teachers in both counties. The programme for these weekends varies — the focus might be to provide opportunities for the writing up of their classroom work, or to develop their own personal writing — but every weekend enables teachers to discuss their work at length with interested colleagues. Participants are assured of respect for their endeavours in an atmosphere which is both critical and supportive. The weekends are demanding as teachers share views and problems, explain and justify, analyse and revise and struggle with new perceptions. But they help to confirm that, although we may not have discovered absolute answers, we are at least addressing important questions. Even more intense reflection occurs at our joint Summer Institutes. These six- to ten-day residential events sustain positive curriculum development and constructive in-service programmes, not just for months, but for years afterwards.

Events organised through the Somerset project have created further interest. A Young Writers' Conference created a focus for children as writers, and brought children together from different parts of the county. This conference gave them the chance to discuss their writing processes, to share their writing and to discover the wider network of writers in the county. An event was also organised for teachers who had not previously worked on the project. Presentations were given by project teachers, and visitors gained an insight into some successful strategies.

We have always believed that the most effective way of developing classroom practice is to create opportunities for practising teachers to work with one another inside the classroom as well as outside it. We were able to offer mini-secondments of one day a week to some teachers for one term. Drawn from the local workshop groups, these teachers have worked with one or two colleagues from that same group, spending half or a whole day in that colleague's classroom. The shared investigation into some aspect of writing and learning development has been very productive, both for the project and for the individuals involved — so much so that we have succeeded in extending the programme into the next year. The results of these collaborations are being written up and will make an important addition to our list of publications.

Our principal means of dissemination has been through newsletters and booklets written by teachers and co-ordinators. Initially, teachers were doubtful about the value of their own classroom work and its potential interest for others. Having a range of publications has enabled them to 'start small' and, with increasing confidence, approach the writing of a booklet, perhaps in collaboration with others. The interest shown, especially in the booklets, has done much to raise awareness of the project across these and other LEAs, giving status to the pupils' work, to the teachers concerned and to the changes they have initiated.

2 Looking at writing and learning — and how they develop together

A *framework for writing*

Richard Bates

Teachers who have been asked during in-service courses to define the writing process have found the task very difficult. They all used writing a great deal in their lessons and agreed that it permeated the fabric of the school day, but they couldn't get used to the idea that writing involved a process. One source of that difficulty was a lack of a vocabulary; we didn't have the words to describe what went on when children wrote; there didn't seem to be a metalanguage available. Individuals were stressing the importance of the writing process — James Britton *et al* wrote *'In concerning ourselves with writing as a process, we are suggesting that such a perspective is of major importance in understanding how children's writing develops. . .'*[1] — but ideas about how this might be translated into activities for children seem to evaporate before they reach the classroom. Many teachers were still primarily concerned with the final outcome of the writing process — the writing produced and handed in for marking. They were more interested in what children wrote than in how they went about writing.

What, then, is meant by 'the writing process', and why is an understanding of it important? The process, or framework for writing, which has emerged in Avon during the last three years is this:

- starting writing
- composing
- revising
- editing
- publishing
- evaluating

Teachers' comments about why it is helpful to use such a framework for writing are scattered throughout the rest of this article. One person remarked:

'The way in which they write is the big change. They are more independent now; they take more responsibility for their own work and do it for themselves. This is true even for Infants.'

One aspect of the success of the National Writing Project has been that it has disseminated ideas about the writing process to teachers in classrooms, allowing them to discover for themselves the importance of such a perspective. As well as making established ideas more widely available, the Project has helped teachers to refine and develop their own thinking. Activities which commonly occur when people write have been identified, and those activities have been further scrutinised. This, of course, is not to say that a new way of teaching writing has been discovered. Much as I would like to think we were in the vanguard of educational thought, it is closer to the truth to say that we have gathered together elements of good classroom practice and tried to put them into a framework for writing which can be easily understood by teachers and young writers. An important feature of the Project's work is that the process is made explicit to children and the language made available to them, so they can discuss their own and each other's writing within that context. We are not, of course, suggesting that there is only one way to teach writing; that would be dangerous, as all institutionalised orthodoxy is dangerous. Within the basic framework, many teaching approaches are possible.

Whatever the approach, and whatever the task, it is clear that if writers are given a vocabulary with which to describe what they are doing, if they can think about writing in terms of smaller and much more manageable activities, they are more likely to be in control of what they are doing.

'Less confident writers are able to produce better writing. The process approach has helped them particularly. They write for longer; they have more stamina because it is more interesting for them.'

If teachers have a vocabulary with which to discuss writing (other than the vocabulary which highlights the surface features of writing such as spelling and punctuation) their response to children's texts will be more informed and helpful. For example, to say to a writer that a piece of writing had not been successfully edited and that many good ideas had been lost between brainstorming and publication because the revision group's ideas were not incorporated, is more helpful than the familiar *'poor spelling, try harder next time'*.

The Avon framework for writing was generated in three important ways: (a) teachers observing children writing and talking to them about how they went about it; (b) teachers writing themselves and reflecting on the processes they went through;

(c) teachers reading about the work of other writing projects, especially those in the USA, Canada and Australia.

'Infants are not drawing first and then writing about it. They're now writing first and illustrating that writing. That has been the big change for me; they see themselves as writers.'

Our framework has much in common with other models. There are slight differences; for example, 'drafting' has been refined into 'composing' and 'revising'. (Children seem to find it easier to understand composing to be the initial attempt to put ideas together, and revising to be a revisiting of those ideas to see if they sound right. For some children, drafting has connotations of *'doing it in rough and writing it up in neat'*.) Also, 'conferencing' has been abandoned by many teachers because they feel that to have a specific moment within the process (conferencing usually comes after revising) when the pupil and teacher sit down to talk about the work is too artificial and impractical. Teachers often identify other moments when they need to intervene in the process.

'The children organise themselves more, asking questions: "What am I doing next?" "Where am I in the process?" They ask each other. Writing has become more noisy and collaborative, it's become like a workshop.'

The starting writing stage includes activities such as brainstorming, note-taking, flow diagrams and finding a focus. If writers are going to be able to construct texts independently they need access to a number of strategies. How do you take notes? In what ways is taking notes from a speaker different from taking notes from a book? How can brainstorming help a writer who is finding it difficult to start? What is the place of journals and writing folders? It is in the context of the starting writing stage that all these issues can be raised.

'The concentration span has increased; the children are more engaged and engrossed.'

During the composing stage, meaning begins to take shape on the paper. The writer need not be concerned with accuracy in surface features; that comes later during the editing stage. At the composing stage, writers may continue to gather information and make decisions about the focus of their writing. (This is, of course, much easier to do if the purpose of the writing is clear and the writer has a specific audience in mind.)

The revising stage may occur after a break of a day or two. It is the time to look afresh at the writing produced so far and ask the questions: *'Have I said what I had intended?' 'Does it make sense?' 'Does it sound right?'* The best way to answer these questions is often to share the work (reading it to a small group for their response). Revising does not

mean writing it out neatly; it involves a fundamental reorganisation of the text, elaborating (or omitting) details and clarifying the meaning of particular sentences or passages. When the writer is satisfied that the meaning of the writing is clear (that it has fulfilled its purpose for the specific audience and is in an appropriate format) it is time to edit the writing.

'There is more co-operation in the class now; they accept criticism from each other and at the same time they are more self-critical, for example, when they reflect on their own work or read it through after it has been published. They never read through their work before, it was finished and over — "let's get on to the next piece . . ."'

The editing stage is where the technical aspects of the children's work are improved. Project teachers have encouraged children to examine surface features only at the editing stage, thus freeing the writer to concentrate on content, style and organisation in previous stages. There are many possible approaches; some teachers use the occasion to group round them writers with a particular problem (perhaps use of the capital letter to mark the beginning of a new sentence, or speech marks) and members of the group will edit each other's work, focusing only on that particular aspect of editing. On other occasions, groups of children will edit each other's work completely, perhaps in a coloured pencil. To identify which child did what to which text, they would initial in the same colour at the bottom of the page. A common activity would be for the groups to edit each other's work, collaborating and learning from each other. This is a marked shift from the teacher collecting the work and proof-reading it. The teacher's role is now effectively to model the editing activity. One way of doing this is to write a short piece, with errors in it, on an overhead projector. The class (or group) would be asked to help with editing the work; they usually delight in finding the mistakes.

'They have more sense of the whole story . . . they don't make it up as they go along . . . they know how it's going to end . . . it's planned.'

Publishing is an important stage in the writing process because it provides a focal point, a product in which the writer can take pride and pleasure. It also allows children to reach a wide audience with their writing — perhaps through the class or school library — in the form of an oral report, a play, a discussion, a presentation or a tape recording. Publishing also offers the opportunity to discuss illustrations and layout, and may be the time to focus on handwriting, typing or word processing.

Collections of children's published work can be used for formative evaluation and allow children to see their own development as writers. Evaluation is encouraged throughout the process, not simply on the final product. *'Am I good at revising?'* is as important a question as *'Am I a good speller?'*

'The children read the teacher's comments differently now. The comment is part of a dialogue and they often respond to it — sometimes just with a written "Yes" or "No", but sometimes with longer comments.'

Again it needs emphasising that there is no suggestion that writers should always go through all these stages every time they construct a text. There are many occasions when it would be inappropriate to do so (writing a note to the milkman, diary entries). The stages are recursive. When I am editing my writing for publication, new ideas often occur to me, or I will think of a better way of expressing an idea. Writing is an activity through which meanings become clear to the writer during the course of the writing process; they are not stacked in the mind and tipped on to the page in sequence. The instruction to write *straight into best books; get it finished in twenty minutes so I can mark it at home* needs close examination.

A process-based approach encourages teachers to look at the way in which children write, rather than at their finished texts. Teachers who have introduced a process-based approach to the teaching of writing typically identify these sorts of benefit to children:

- opportunities to develop their own writing and take responsibility for it

- enthusiasm for writing

- a commitment to make their writing better

- the confidence which comes from having control over the system

- self-management and motivation

- increased involvement in the tasks, particularly when the children have instigated them

- the 'new' language for discussing writing

'The children engage more personally in the writing now. In Maths they might write "I don't really understand this work — it's hard" or at the end of a piece of writing they may say "This isn't my best work — I wasn't in the mood when I wrote this". This probably comes from their use of journals as think books, but it spills over into other areas. They know writing is for communication and they want to tell you what is on their mind. The relationship is different — they want you to know.'

References

[1] James Britton *et al*: *The Development of Writing Abilities 11-18* (Macmillan 1975)

Whose language?

Barbara Grayson

Suppose for a moment that you were confronted by a competition tie-breaker that began: *'Children develop as effective writers when . . .'*

How could you complete the sentence? It is possible that your ideas may look something like this:

'. . . they are encouraged to draw on the knowledge they gain about literacy from their environment and from the more experienced writers they observe'

'. . . they are given opportunities to explore a wide variety of formats and styles of writing and to make decisions about how to write appropriately for different purposes and audiences'

'. . . they see that writing can be a tool for gaining a greater understanding of experiences and knowledge that are unique to themselves, and that it can help them to represent this understanding to others'

You might even win the competition. If the statements not only represent potential competition winners, but also reflect the opportunities you actually provide in your classroom, your pupils have a good chance of developing as effective and confident writers — at least in Standard English, which is the dominant medium for learning and literacy in British schools.

When we make these statements, whom do we have in mind? Is it that almost mythical person — the monolingual, monodialectal user of Standard English? What of the greater number of children who have access through their homes and communities to dialects and languages other than Standard English? How do we apply our statements to them? Are they being given opportunities to draw on all their experiences of spoken and written language? Are we encouraging them to explore the whole range of styles and forms of writing available to them? Do they feel able to engage with their differing cultural experiences and understandings through their writing? In short — is value being given to their range of language forms and cultural experiences, or are they being devalued by omission? Are we doing less than our best for our pupils' personal growth and academic progress?

Many of us — both adults and children — use and understand forms of language other than Standard English. Even those of us who see ourselves as essentially monolingual know that we can vary our language to suit the situation. With our family and friends, we may use regional words or phrases, which we would avoid in, for instance, a job interview. Children are likely to talk differently to their friends in the playground and to their teachers in the classroom. We recognise that we may construct written language differently from spoken language. Those of us who speak different dialects and languages know that we have an even wider choice of language forms, and again we use them as seems appropriate to the situation, the ideas we wish to express and the people we are talking with or writing for.

The resentment and frustration generated when teachers deny the validity of this experience of language outside school can be seen in this reflection from a Secondary school pupil in Rotherham:

'Yes, teachers always correct the way I speak and also the way I write. They mainly correct the way I write more than anything. When I write a story and I include talking I write it how I would speak. But sometimes teachers cross it out and put in how they would talk. I don't think they should do that, they should leave it as it is.'

Many pupils are left to struggle with social and academic uncertainties, and pressures caused by conflicting experiences of language use which school intensifies rather than resolves. A British-born Afro-Caribbean student described the discrepancies he observed between the way he spoke at home, and the way he was required to speak and write at school, particularly in order to pass exams. When asked by Beryle Jones whether he agreed with the switch he had to make, he said:

'I don't really agree with it but I can't be against that because it's England, it's their country . . . but if . . . ' (pause) 'it's their language, but if I was to go to the West Indies and I was to write West Indian dialect I'd most probably pass, but over here . . .'

As Beryle commented, *'The fact that the student is wrong in his assumptions about the likely acceptance of his own use of language in the West Indies does not minimise his own personal struggle and sense of contradiction.'*

A class of Junior children in East London collected information about the languages that they wrote and spoke, and presented their findings on a bar chart (right).

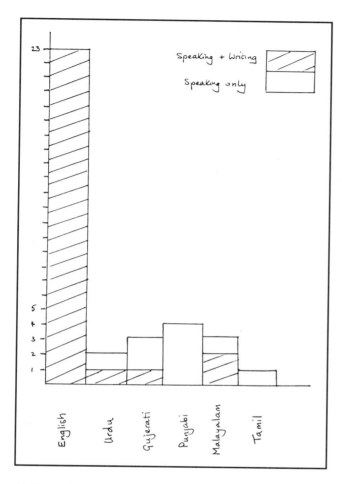

Half the class speak at least two languages, but very few of them are literate in a language other than English. What opportunities are they missing in not being able to develop all the forms of literacy available to them?

If we are to help children become effective and confident writers, we must make it possible for them to build on their whole language repertoire and to feel confident about drawing on their range of cultural experiences.

We know that, from a very early age, children are aware of the literacies around them; they are observing how older and more experienced writers use writing. If they are given opportunities and encouragement, they will experiment with different forms and uses of writing.

Six-year-old Raki draws on her knowledge of three literacy systems — Bengali, Urdu and English. She seems to be quite clear that they are separate systems but that they all have the same function — representing meaning.

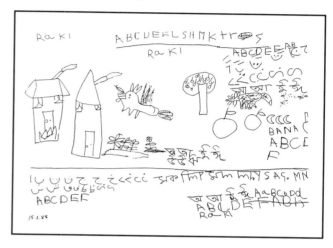

At a later stage of development Rujina is also using two forms of literacy to convey her meaning — this time in a letter to her cousin in Bangladesh. In both Bengali and English she experiments with writing.

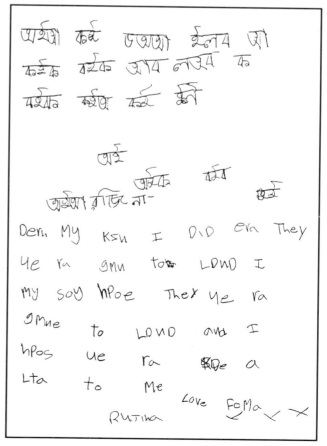

37

Some children may develop strategies which enable them to use one literacy to support another. Wan Leong uses his knowledge of both Cantonese and English to produce a draft which later becomes a final piece in English:

> on Sanday me went to the
> 游泳池 Simming my dad
> want to Simm too. mum is
> eating 蘋果 in b he
> 游泳池
>
>   Wan-Leong
>
> On Sunday I went to the
> sea-side to Simm my dad
> want to Simm too mum is
> eating an apple at the
> sea-side and I just Simm.

Kalpana is a Secondary pupil, recently arrived in England. Already literate in Gujarati, she used her existing literacy to support her new one in order to write a diary as part of her GCSE course in Child Development. A year later her English was considered strong enough for her to be entered for seven GCSEs, and undoubtedly her confidence in using one language to support the second had contributed to her rapid development.

> After noon
> 1. o'clock children come
> [Gujarati text] started
> windy housing bot [Gujarati text]
> [Gujarati text] chair [Gujarati text]
> [Gujarati text] black ball [Gujarati text]
> [Gujarati text] shapes [Gujarati text] Wood
> work [Gujarati text] Children [Gujarati text]
> [Gujarati text]
> [Gujarati text]

Children who have become confident and competent users of more than one form of spoken and written language are able to make choices about how they will use these, bearing in mind the effect they wish to achieve and their intended audience. The children at the Rustam Iranian School in

London embarked on a fundraising project to support an Iranian child who needed a major operation. As well as raising money, they wished to extend their support by writing to both the boy and his parents. The pupils themselves decided on the activities that were needed, and chose the appropriate language for their writing. Should posters be in Farsi or English? What about the letters?

The effectiveness of the voice in the following piece would have been lost if the writer had not been able to choose a linguistic form other than Standard English:

> If this world was mine
> I'd play RUBA DUB all the time
> I'll play it ina one style
> I'll play it till the
> morning light ,
> Till the people dem get up bright .
> Ah , Ah , Ah , Ah .
>
> The girls dem see me from afar
> Some of them call me SUPERSTAR
> But when I was a yout'
> Dem say fly a follow me batty
> But now me is a man
> Dem want a remedy
> Fe make dem feel Irei
>
> Me seh me Know a little yout'
> By de name of Billy Bwoy
> Him take a little trip
> Down to Mexico
> And change his name to
> BILLY BWOYO
> 'Cu Billy Bwoyo won't make
> you bad so
> Me say him have two big sister
> And dem kill him brother
> 'cause him a work obiah .

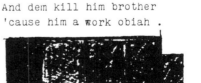

Other children have taken account of the languages spoken by different children in the intended audience for their writing, and have provided bilingual texts.

Writing is not, however, merely a matter of linguistic forms: nor does it take place in a vacuum. Writers operate within, and wish to find means of expressing, their own particular cultural and social experiences. Bilingual and bidialectal writers are bicultural writers. They have access to a wider variety of experience than a monolingual writer and it is important that children in school should feel able to draw on this experience. They may wish to site their writing within a particular culture, or they may wish to make their own synthesis of different experiences and ways of making meaning.

In the process of writing an information book about Hinduism, a group of Hindu children in a Birmingham Junior school had to research their community's religion, languages and culture since their knowledge, as eleven-year-olds, was partial and limited. They gained a more firmly grounded view of themselves and of their community through this experience — particularly the boys, who seemed to hold more ambivalent views than the girls and who had been more influenced by the dominance of the language and culture of the wider community. One boy commented that when he went to Secondary school the following year, he would probably choose to take Punjabi as a modern language option beause he now knew quite a lot about it.

When Firdous and Fatima were given the opportunity to write a story for other Bengali-speaking children, they were able to draw on experiences and knowledge that made their writing come alive. They drew on cultural customs and Bengali vocabulary because they knew their audience would understand them:

Then she went and knocked on the door. Their anutie opened the door and said "come in! The anutie was called anutie Rukia, she was very rich. She had a very big house in Chittagong but she had no children of her own. She tried lots of times to have a Baby (adopted) but she had no baby. Nazma and Ripa peeped through the window and then their anutie (chachi) called them to come in and have some tea and Mishti (sweets) and samosa. When they were eating mishti and samosa their chachi said I have some thing to tell you! Your new anutie Rukia has no children and she asked me if she can have Nazma to live with her in chittagong and I said yes". Then Nazma and Ripa started to cry! "Why does Nazma have to go and stay with her?" "Because she has no children."

Infant children in Cleveland combined their different experiences of weddings to make a written synthesis of the customs of more than one culture. It gave all the children in the group the opportunity to share, and be confirmed in, the validity of their own home and community experience.

Language, experience and the cultural context in which they are sited are inextricably entwined. We can always write more compellingly about ideas and situations which we have lived through or in some way made our own. Whichever language form bilingual and bidialectal pupils are using, they should feel able to draw on the totality of their experience in their writing. The ethos of the school and the classroom can either help or hinder this choice. Mary Maguire, reflecting on children's perceptions of themselves as writers in a bilingual French/English 'immersion' programme in Quebec, makes the following observation:

'Their decisions to include information and specific features are derived from a complex interplay between their own conceptualisations of the functions of story-making and their teacher's conceptualisations. The patterns I see evolving in the children's perceptions of narrative and narrating in English and French suggest that the differences are not necessarily language-specific but are influenced more by what the child narrator feels licensed to create and what resources he feels he can draw on in the story-making process.' [1]

In all these examples, teachers had a very clear view of the pupils for whom they were making provision — not solely the monolingual, monodialectal speakers of Standard English, but pupils with very different language experiences. They had considered the ethos of their classrooms and the implications of the unspoken messages being transmitted to the children about the value of their language and their culture. They had created an atmosphere in which both adults and children had respect for each other's experiences. Their pupils felt at ease in drawing on all the varieties of language and literacy at their disposal, and were confident that their cultural backgrounds were valid resources for their writing. They had been able to use and build upon all their knowledge of literacy. Their existing written and spoken language competence had been encouraged.

Not all children are willing or able to spend further hours during evenings or at weekends in a community school, and not all have teachers in their mainstream school who know their home or community language. If we accept the validity of supporting children's use of language forms other than Standard English, we must consider the provision we make within schools and within the community for the development of writers literate in more than one language — although there may be enormous difficulties to overcome in relation to attitudes and financial support.

Acknowledgement and thanks are due to the following people who provided the examples used in this article: Jacqui Clover, Manjula Datta, Lorna Drummond, Viv Edwards, Beryle Jones, Joya Knight, Rani Kumar, Margaret J. Meek, Gitika Ray, Sheila Rehman, Joan Sedgewicke, Stewart Trainor, Barbara Walters and Shahila Taheri White.

References

[1] Mary Maguire: 'How do they tell? Écrire c'est choisir' from *Language and Literacy in the Primary School* ed. M. Meek and C. Mills (Falmer Press 1988)

Fitting writing into learning

Sue Horner

One of the principal reasons for pupils to be at school is to learn. Once in school, they write for all sorts of reasons. It is to be hoped, therefore, that at least some of the writing may relate to and assist the learning. This relationship is likely to be determined by the nature of learning as teachers and pupils see it.

'I got them all right!'

'They were really engrossed in what they were doing, and didn't notice the lesson was over.'

'I enjoyed that!'

'This is an excellent piece of work — you've covered all the information and organised it in a logical and interesting way.'

'I never realised that before.'

In class, teachers are constantly assessing the evidence before them to see what progress is being made and whether their pupils might be helped by any adjustments to the task, the groupings, or any other factor. Sometimes noise and excitement are evidence of commitment and involvement; at other times they denote wandering attention and lack of structure. When marking a pile of papers or books, teachers may see untidy notes and jottings as a lack of care and precision, or as a part of the process of thinking or drafting. What teachers count as evidence of learning depends on what they think learning is, and what is appropriate behaviour for learners. Reactions to the evidence depend on the interpretation chosen — whether to continue or to redirect, to demand a rewrite or to encourage interim ideas. Teachers, then, choose courses of action based on various sorts of evidence. Learners may view this evidence differently, and their views will be influenced by their own background and purposes as well as by schools and teachers. They may be very concerned about teacher approval, or want to feel they have acquired some more facts. They may think that being purposefully occupied is not important, or they may attach more value to the chance to say (or write) what they think. Where teachers are not explicit about what is being achieved, learners are likely to rely on criteria from the 'hidden curriculum' or from their own ideas.

The similarities and differences between the perceptions of learners and those of teachers are important. If learners are to have any sense of long-term development, they need to know how particular activities fit into overall schemes. Commitment, interest and achievement are likely to be enhanced when learners understand the answers to questions such as:

- Why am I doing this?

- What am I trying to achieve?

- Who is it for?

- What is the best way for me to set about it?

If the answers to questions such as these are not explicitly discussed, learners are left to infer — from the task, from previous experience and from teachers' responses — the purposes, the criteria for success and the most appropriate ways of working. If learners are to take more responsibility for their learning, to become more autonomous, these questions must be addressed directly. They are significant whether or not the focus of the work is writing.

One function of writing (which is much used and abused) is to provide evidence of what a writer/ learner knows, understands and can do. This evidence may, of course, vary greatly — from filling in one-word blanks to extensive essay writing, from brief summaries to lengthy evaluations or alternatives. However, it cannot be assumed, for example, that because a pupil has copied accurately from a blackboard or textbook, (s)he has understood and assimilated the information that has been written. Pupils who write up a Science experiment competently or outline the causes of historical events may primarily be demonstrating that they have understood the accepted way of writing in these contexts. There may be only tenuous evidence in the writing that they have grasped the significance of the information and built new insights into their understanding. Teachers may devise structures and patterns for the writing in order to help pupils to think, but it is this very structure which may constrict learning, and may obscure evidence that a process of making new meaning is going on. Where the pattern laid down for the writing is so explicit as to leave little or no choice for the learner, it is not easy to see how this writing can relate positively to the learning process. In these circumstances the learner is disadvantaged, and teacher control may inhibit learning by denying the learner the opportunity to learn while writing. Writing in school tends to happen at the end of a sequence of activities, and so is unlikely to show the process of active meaning making. If pupils are speculating and hypothesising about a topic, and if they are scrutinising their ideas to see whether they work, it is possible that a perambulating teacher may overhear this, but it is not easy to attend to all the pupils in this way. A wider view of writing may help teachers to have more access to the learning. Space to experiment, to make mistakes, to reflect, to choose or to pursue particular interests may be offered; when learners use writing to help them in these activities, it is not just the chore that follows the learning.

The relationship between writing and learning, then, is not straightforward. Groups of teachers who have grappled with this have commented that learning itself is a 'slippery concept' — it is a complicated process, idiosyncratic, unpredictable and hard to define. It is therefore important to attempt to pin down this concept, so that writing may be examined alongside it. These teachers did identify some crucial elements of learning:

> *Learning is:*
>
> a constructive process, making connections, building on the old, making sense of the new, developing and extending awareness, knowledge, experience, skills, concepts
>
> *Learning involves:*
>
> — selecting
> — empathising
> — reflecting
> — imagining
> — analysing
> — hypothesising
> — classifying
> — evaluating
> — visualising
> — organising

The classroom tasks and activities which promote learning processes such as these are likely to involve talking, doing and writing, as well as reading, watching and listening. Learners need opportunities to reflect on what they are and have been doing, and to consider effective ways of working. For example: Is it helpful to make a few notes before discussing? Is it useful to predict beforehand what might happen, so that shifts of understanding may be perceived? Is it sensible to discuss findings before committing them to paper?

If learners can see connections between the learning process and what they actually do, they are more likely to be able to make appropriate choices on another occasion.

Connections also need to be made between recognising what has been learned and knowing what the learner can then do with it. If learners are able to recognise what they are learning, the ways in which they are learning, and what they are then enabled to do, they are likely to be able to proceed when a new challenge is encountered. The ways of working are then used when there is a new demand for them.

If we try to specify exactly what is going on when learners are at work, there is a danger of becoming overprescriptive and dogmatic about how learning does and should happen. The elements of learning identified above all imply that learners bring with them views, knowledge, understanding and emotions which are the results of previous experience. When presented with new tasks, ideas

and problems, learners generalise from previous experience and begin to hypothesise about the new. When predictions are proved right and new ideas fit with previous patterns, the learners' ideas are confirmed and learning may seem easy. When new experiences do not readily fit categories the learner has worked out, more strategies are needed to engage with the new, so that the learner grasps the new ideas and takes control of them. These strategies may include imagining, evaluating, analysing and reorganising, to link the old and the new and to find a way of handling the new.

A learner in a classroom may be presented with topic headings such as 'The Vikings', 'The properties of symmetry' or 'Myths and legends'. If the learner is to integrate new learning with what is already understood, it is important to recollect previous relevant experiences and relate them to these topics. These recollections may include a visit to the Jorvic Museum in York; or a kaleidoscope once owned; or stories full of beasts and fantasies told by a grandmother.

If these connections are not made, the learner is much less likely to grasp the significance of new learning or to adjust previous ideas. What happens in the classroom is likely to be seen as something quite different from what is already known from other sources and experiences.

Teachers are familiar with a wide range of ways of gaining pupils' interest and setting up tasks which invite worthwhile thought and effort. The necessary relating of previous knowledge to the current topic in the classroom may be explicitly invited by the teacher, or may happen as work proceeds. For example, for the topic 'The Vikings', it would be possible for an introduction to include:

- reading a story with a relevant setting

- setting the problem of how to design a ship for the invasion of Britain

- asking questions about how the Vikings lived

- considering invasions and invaders

Similarly, when thinking about 'the properties of symmetry' the teacher might:

- set up a series of experiments for pupils to conduct and then reflect on

- show and discuss various types of symmetrical design

- invite pupils to think about mirror images

The way a topic is introduced affects the sequence of learning activities undertaken by learners. In particular, it influences the occasions when reflection, generalisation or evaluation may be relevant, although all of these are likely to be needed at times.

This chart suggests how different routes will tend to have elements in common.

Setting a problem	Creating images	Questions
for example, design and make a model of a ship	*for example, reading a story or a novel*	*for example, how did the Vikings live?*
What do I know about this?	What seems important about this?	What do I already know which seems relevant?
What seem to be the main lines of enquiry?	What else does it prompt me to think/find out?	What else do I need to find out?
What do I need in order to proceed?	How shall I set about it?	How can I follow this up?
	What resources are available?	
	What have I found out?	
	What does it mean?	
	How does it relate to where I started from and where I've been?	
	How would I sum up what I've learned (and present it to others)?	
	Where might I go next?	

Although this sequence of questions is apparently linear, it is likely that at any point a learner will backtrack, project ahead, be distracted, or, for various reasons, fail to reach a point where achievement and understanding are consolidated or are evidently under control.

One important source of support is other learners. Although the process outlined above is an individualised one, much is learned through and with other learners. They may complement each other, ask each other questions, test each other's ideas and help each other in looking for answers. The potential of collaboration in learning should not be underestimated.

Other elements of an environment supportive to learners are ones over which teachers have a large measure of influence. Teachers can provide freedom within structure, offer models as well as opportunities, challenge as well as encourage. It is vital to help learners to be explicit about what they are learning and how they are setting about it. Learners need to understand that they have a range of strategies available when tackling tasks and that they can control the process.

This is summed up in the chart on the right:

Learners need...	
... to be:	*... and to:*
— confident	— have a repertoire of motivated ways of working
— persistent	— have control of their language
— curious	— be self-critical
— patient	— recognise that learning is a variable process
— open	— value themselves
	— believe what they are doing is worthwhile
	— have a sense of purpose

A helpful environment includes:

support, encouragement

success, challenge

opportunities to articulate, experiment, reflect, make mistakes

freedom to choose, initiate, follow up interests

structures, including models, ways of working, guidance

others, to collaborate with, to share experiences

Writing which accompanies learning activities is likely to look different from that which comes at the end because it serves different purposes. As learners proceed they may find writing useful for recording ideas and information, trying out connections, crystallising their ideas, noting something for use later, communicating with someone else, and for many other purposes. Writing which comes at the end may help the learner to sum up what has been happening and what has been learned, but this writing is dependent on and is a part of the process, not an afterthought.

This chart shows how different kinds of writing may be useful at different stages of the learning process. The learning strategies are used by learners as appropriate, and those mentioned here are suggestions rather than prescriptions.

Tasks	Learning strategies	What the writing looks like
Early grappling with a problem/issue/question	Classifying, imagining, recalling, questioning, ordering existing knowledge	Notes anecdotes, lists, ideas
Deciding what to do	Defining, hypothesising, ordering priorities, organising	Questions, statements, plans, drafts
Working on the topic	Recording, observing, analysing, selecting, modifying	Notes, diagrams, tables, records, changes of plan
Finishing off, presenting findings and ideas	Categorising, evaluating, concluding, summarising	A wide range of forms

Approached in this way, writing gives access to the learning process, for both the learner and the teacher. It enables the learner to trace the work back to the beginning, to see how early ideas have been modified in the light of subsequent events and to see progress and achievement, as well as critically to analyse difficulties and failures. The final presentation, written or oral, may give the teacher a sense of what has been done or learned, but scrutiny of the earlier, interim writing will help clarify crucial issues, such as whether pupils are valuing what they bring to the classroom, whether they find questioning and hypothesising easy, or whether they use their observations and analysis effectively when working towards conclusions. This kind of insight, a new sort of classroom evidence, provides an agenda for further teaching which is rather different from that which derives from identifying items of content which have not yet been grasped.

The teacher then needs to rethink the proposition *'Writing will help me to assess whether they've learned what I wanted them to'*, so that it becomes *'Writing will help them learn (along with talking and doing) what I want them to'*.

These processes of writing and learning must be made explicit to the learners too. This gives them the confidence to tackle new topics, and the realisation that learning is a constructive process over which they may take control.

Writing demands in Science

Jeremy Tafler

Is Science writing different from writing in other subjects? Many of us might feel that in some way it is, that the whole nature of the scientific method (whatever that is) demands an approach to language which has a unique set of rules and values. I suggest that this claim to the special case is overstated.

In Science, words do assume meanings which are subtly different from those of everyday life, and this is a source of profound misunderstanding, especially amongst Secondary pupils, However, writing in Science is not a separate sort of writing, a separate genre; it comes in all sorts of different guises, overlapping with writing in other areas.

It is obvious that pieces of work with different purposes and audiences will look different. An expressive poem and an account of an experiment will demand very different styles, but so would an expressive poem and an account of the causes and effects of the Industrial Revolution. It is part of our role as teachers to provide pupils with a range of experiences which will allow them to select and use the most suitable strategies and modes of expression. There is a whole range of different types of Science writing determined by purpose and audience, just as there should be in other subjects across the curriculum.

What is the Science writing stereotype? How might we describe two extremes of school writing, exemplified in English and Science?

Science

objective, dispassionate, general, non-observer-dependent

English

subjective, engaged, anecdotal, expressive, personal

Are these stereotypes repeated outside the school classroom?

One preoccupation of teachers in Science lessons is the ubiquitous 'write-up'. The old orthodoxy is somewhat discredited, but it still has wide currency.

Here is a traditional format for an account of an experiment:

1 Title/aim

2 Diagram

3 Method

4 Results/observations

5 Conclusion

The words may change, but simply substituting *'hypothesis'* for *'aim'* and *'pattern'* for *'conclusion'* does not, of itself, demonstrate a change of practice. In the past, learners were frequently provided with this template as simply the accepted way in which

write-ups had to be done. The justification of writing up was often simply to promote the 'skill' of writing up itself. Success was gauged by how successfully the pupil achieved the teacher's ideal, and the teacher was sole arbiter of this. Pupils seldom had the chance to experiment with different formats, to write for a real purpose or an audience other than the teacher, to have access to other means of gauging success or to write for reasons other than to learn how to. I would suggest that this attitude is:

- unproductive; it distances children from their own work and thus prevents the internalisation of ideas

- unsupported; take a look at the workbooks of real scientists — there's not much sign of this style of writing there

- ineffective; write-ups frequently do not demonstrate the qualities that we are seeking

Let us leave write-ups for a moment and make a more general claim. Writing is not given sufficient priority in Science lessons. The problem is not that we set too little of it (probably the reverse), but that it is not sufficiently exploited to do the things that it can do uniquely well. Too much Science writing is of questionable value, giving pupils little opportunity for rehearsal of new ideas and wider explorations of what they actually think. All too often the writing seems to be some vague ritual, whose purpose is lost in the distant past and certainly lost on the pupils.

Here is a brief attempt to elaborate the uses to which writing can be put in Science lessons:

1 To communicate what is known

- to the teacher

- to others

2 As a tool for learning

- What does the learner think?

- How can the thinking develop?

3 To reflect on learning

- to look at the process of learning

- to be self-critical

- to look at the reason for believing one thing rather than another

- to make implicit knowledge explicit

1 To communicate what is known . . . to the teacher

In discussions with other teachers, this is perhaps the most commonly stated reason for filling up exercise books. But how effectively do the set tasks

45

allow the teacher to find out what the writer actually knows and understands? And how much time (and interest) do you have in reading thirty accounts of how oxygen is transported in the blood?

To cite an example:[1]

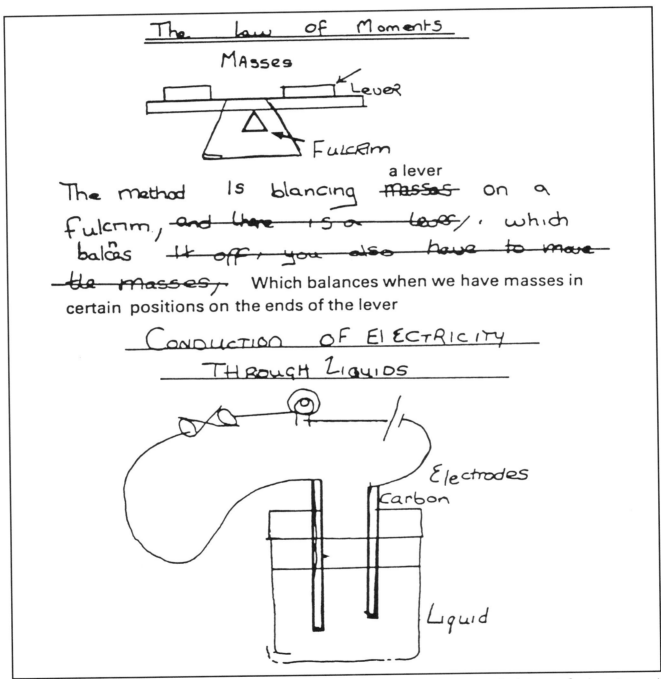

(print = teacher's responses)

As the authors state, in this carefully corrected exercise there is little opportunity for the fifteen-year-old writer to engage in her work. It is difficult to know what she is thinking, what her perceived models are. The other thirty accounts in the class were very similar.

Compare the piece on the right, taken from the same source. This work was done by twelve-year-olds whose task was to work out how they might produce fresh water if they were stranded on a mountain. It was made clear to the pupils that they could select their own format — for example, they could write a story if they wished.

Wanted — Distilled Water. 1d.pp. — Halfway up a mountain — 3000 miles from nowhere.

Jacobs was desperately ill. The only cure was distilled water. We had a primus stove. a few empty bottles and a kettle. All our food consisted of was a few dry biscuits and the remains of the cake. We had a tent and a blanket. "Suprizingly little", you may think for such a large expedition. Most of our gear had been lost in a blizzard. Snow lay thick all about us. In fact, it nearly covered us. We huddled together around Jacobs trying in vain to think of a way to get the water that Jacobs so desperately needed. Blitzen suddenly jumped up, smacked his head on the tent roof and yelled "I have it!". He told us that when he was at school it had been a hard winter, and the teacher had demonstrated how to get distilled water from snow. First you had to light the primus and hang over it a kettle cram-packed with snow. When the snow had melted and began to boil you had to catch the steam in the a

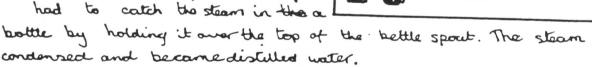

bottle by holding it over the top of the kettle spout. The steam condensed and became distilled water.

We set to work at once. Jacobs was in a really bad way. We found that we had to change the bottles over rather frequently to get the maximum amount of water. Soon we had to empty the first bottles into a second bottle because the water ran out if we gathered too much at once. It was a long time before we had enough water to meet our needs. Jacobs was in a fever. As the water passed between his lips he sank back into a world of relief. We persisted in making as much as possible of the distilled water because it looked as though there would soon be another blizzard. A few days later Jacobs recovered. We had done it!

It may be argued that *'to communicate with the teacher'* can become so dominant a rationale that any other use of writing is forgotten.

To communicate what is known . . . to others

We all need to communicate. Our ultimate aim is to communicate effectively, concisely and without ambiguity (this includes spelling and neatness). There is no disagreement about this. People do disagree, however, about how to make learners more confident and accomplished in their communication. It seems clear that the communicator needs to have something worth communicating to an audience which is interested (at least potentially) in what the communicator has to say, and which is preferably accessible to the communicator.

There is nothing dramatic or revolutionary about this. In Waingels Copse School in Berkshire, the National Writing Project co-ordinator, Audrey Gregory, was working with teachers and children following a traditional Chemistry course. Working first on 'Iron and steel' and then on 'Pollution', the group divided to allow pupils to work in smaller groups on a chosen aspect of the topic. After about two weeks the groups had to publish and present their findings to the rest of the class. They had all developed skills and an understanding of underlying processes, but they had covered different content. There was a real reason to communicate their findings to each other — if only so that they could all pass the examination. The write-up of their work was not a pointless, arduous task, but one with real meaning and real motivation.

(The child-centred work on the subject of maggots [p 50] also led naturally to the need to publish.)

Communication should be worthwhile. Often it is sufficient to use the rest of the class as an audience, and all that is necessary is to allow a little variety to make it more interesting.

Here are some more examples of publishing for peers which have allowed learners to put more of themselves into the writing. A fourth year in a Somerset school watched a demonstration of the alkali metals experiment, and chose to write it up in the form of a poem. How does one reconcile the need for objectivity and accuracy with poetic licence?

'The alkali metal experiment

The safety precautions were ready,
Rubber gloves and all,
The people in the front row wore goggles,
It was going to be dangerous for all.

The lithium metal was first,
The tweezers were at the ready,
He pulled it out and chopped it up,
And said, "OK, are you ready?"

It went in the water with a fizz,
It started to let off some gas,
It speeded round the bowl,
As everybody looked and gasped.

The sodium metal was next,
This was going to be better,
We used some different clean water,
And waited for Sir to set it.

It went in the water at once,
From green to blue it went,
Then it turned into a silvery ball,
And turned around and bent.

It fizzed then disappeared,
All rather sudden,
It let off a bit of gas,
Now that experiment was over,
The one I was waiting for —
AT LAST!

Potassium was last and final,
It went in the water with a bang,
It fizzed and let off fire and sparks,
And then the bell rang.

The potassium was the most dangerous,
Sir let it off then ran,
He said if you held this metal,
It would burn straight through your hand.

I looked but I stood well away
I'd rather not be blown up, you see,
It looked pretty dangerous,
And I want my eyesight to see.'

Susan Horvetty

Here are some more examples of children's write-ups, this time from Primary schools.

How To Make a string telephone

1. You heD a ParTner.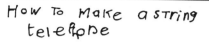

2 two yoghurt cartons

3 Get Some scissors anD makea hole in them.

4 snaP a mach STick

5. Get Some sTring anD Put The match ih The Hole

6. PuT The STring iN The Hole anD Tie it To the mateh.

iT DiD work

iT WorkeD BesT with The STrihg Tight

it WorKeD round a corner.

PLASTICINE   CLASS 7

We made a tower and mine was the tallest and then we made a pattern on the plasticine and we were alloud to use anything in the room and I used a screwdriver. I made my tower stand up by putting a pencil by it.
Luke Wilson

Which shape goes the fathest
We made a ramp out of a very big book and I made a sphere first and Ruth went first and I had a orange sphere and Ruths sphere went the fathest and mine was just behind Adis and when Alex had a turn his fell off because It was a cylinder and It kept going different ways.
I got one straw cut up and then I made two spheres and I put them on the strawsand then I put It on the slope and then I let go of It but It went side ways and then I made a flat shape and I put it on its side and I rolled it down the slope but it went side ways instead of straight ahead.

The spheres went the farthest.

Lisa Windebank.

CHANGING SHAPE WITH PLASTICINE

As well as the rest of the class, there are other audiences which can provide a test for the learner's thinking — parents, other classes, other schools, local media. The more these real, responsive audiences are used, the greater the motivation for the pupils to think carefully about what they are trying to do.

2 As a tool for learning: What does the learner think? How can the thinking develop?

We may not know what we think until we talk about it or write it down. Structuring ideas, making sense of them for ourselves, is part of learning. Certain strategies can help with this; one is brainstorming at the beginning of a piece of work, to explore what the learners already know, to put the work into context, to remind the pupils that it is their development that is important and fully to involve the learners in the learning process.

A class was working on the subject of maggots. The pupils brainstormed what they knew, writing down ideas as fast as they could, uncritically.

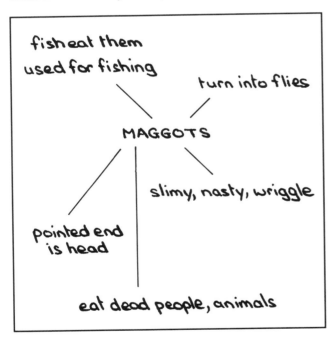

The children then formed pairs and, after sharing their knowledge, decided what areas they would like to find out about. The children then reformed into groups of four, five or six, and, again after sharing, they negotiated a two-week scheme of investigation. They had to write operational plans. The teacher gathered the groups together and produced a wall chart of the areas of interest:

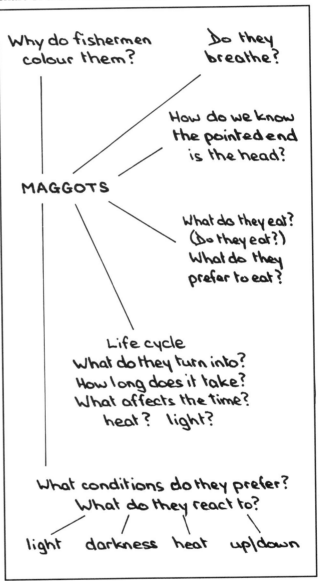

With minimal manipulation he made sure that the projects were possible and reasonable. The investigations might involve book work, experiments or questions to experts. The groups ended up with a range of activities firmly rooted in the children's knowledge, experience and interests, and also, incidentally, covering a large chunk of the Biology syllabus.

From this point on, the class conducted their own research, along similar lines to the Berkshire work mentioned above.

Another strategy which teachers have found helpful is the use of journals or learning logs. There are many different forms of journal, but essentially they are places where a child can jot down ideas and questions, possibly for sharing with the teacher, about what they do and what they do not understand. The teacher responds if requested to, but only to the content of the journal, never to the manner of presentation. The journal belongs to and is under the control of the pupil.

Here are some journal entries from the Mid Glamorgan Writing Project's 'Writing in Primary Science':

> I think that the ballon will shrink because when you put a bottle top under hot water it expands So I thought that when you put the balloon under cold water it will do the oppersite

Today we had an art straw each, and we cut them in to thirds. We flattened about 3cm on one end, and cut the corners off, so the end was pointed. We blew air into them, and some of us made a musical note. Some of us did! I didn't.

We twisted the ends, and Richard made some really musical notes. I think Stuart was the champion blower. Nichola made a scale of five notes. Paul Lewis managed to blow through a plastic drinking straw. Because it was plastic, he cut some holes in it. It took quite a lot of breath to blow a note, but he managed it. Meanwhile, I was still trying.

Nichola started to play, "Amazing Grace," but after the first few notes she couldn't blow anymore. Jemma used a whole art straw and got a base note. Mrs. Rosenfeld said we could make an orchestra! Yes, you can guess, I still couldn't make a note.

Finally, I actually got a note! It was only a very slight squeak, but atleast it was a note. Mind you, it's all I got after half an hour of trying. Mrs Rosenfeld decided to give a prize to Stuart. She gave him a badge from the Police Museum in Bridgend

When we look at children's writing, we often act as though it is sufficient for us to know what is wrong with it and give the child (in the time available to us) a grade to denote the level of success. Generally speaking, though, it is more important for learners to know how successful their strategies have been, and to have confirmation that their knowledge, purposes and skills are tested. Hence the use of journals, learning logs, writing for real audiences (who react), response partners (who criticise), designing something and seeing whether it works, and doing tasks which allow room for personal experimentation.

How often have we, as teachers, constructed an impeccable sequence of ideas, defined the problems, set the practical work, told the children to carry it out, elicited conclusions . . . knowing, in the end, that we have impinged on the learners' mental models not at all? What seems to be important is moving the focus of control at least some way towards the learner and away from the teacher. Writing is an excellent vehicle for problem defining, planning, experimenting and simply working out ideas under the active guidance (not domination) of the teacher.

Even the need to provide revision notes cannot justify the amount of dictation and textbook copying which we have allowed in the past. If revision notes are necessary, perhaps they belong in a separate book with separate rules.

3 To reflect on learning

Perhaps one of the most valuable attributes for the scientist (or the scientific way of looking at things) is scepticism — not always believing the obvious, distrusting one's own eyes, not jumping too hastily to conclusions. How much do we practise what we preach? How often do we, on the contrary, demand acceptance of our world view, and even the language of our world view, because we are the experts?

Opportunities for pupils to interrogate their own views can be provided through class or small group discussion, but why waste so much writing time on copying out other people's facts (ours) in other people's language? Getting it right on paper is not the same as changing what goes on in the mind. If the neat work in the exercise book, complete with pretty diagrams and shading, is what some of our

students need for security, shouldn't we ask ourselves why?

What can we do? We can let them record the development of their thinking, remembering that whereas we may not believe that their ideas are more valid than ours, they are certainly more relevant as a starting point for their development. We can look at the way in which real scientists work, not merely pick out the bits which, out of context, confirm our own school ideas. What was Galileo's world view? How do real scientists write? (Look at the notebooks of Faraday or Davy.) How did the work on the double helix by Watson, Crick and Thomson develop? How scientific is science fiction? Our pupils should learn how real scientists behave rather than merely acquiring an abstract set of skills and knowledge.

In conclusion

These examples, representative of only the first steps in changing the writing diet, show that a more productive use of writing is possible. Writing has not always been used as a method of developing understanding, and the tasks set have not always been suited to the purpose. Sometimes, significantly, the writing has been suited to the purpose but that purpose was not all that it might have been. Science writing in classroms often suggests a view of Science which is not only alienating but also inaccurate. It may service the most repetitive of scientific work and may need to be learned as a vocational skill by those contemplating employment in a laboratory, but there is no case for that sort of Science to make up a fifth of the core curriculum. During the last two decades, the idea has gained ground that not only is it difficult to support the idea of the scientific method, but also it is difficult to describe a scientific method unambiguously and prescriptively.

What sort of language skills, then, do we demand of scientists? It may be argued that we are not really talking about producing Einsteins. Nor, though, are we talking about producing mere jobbing scientists. Science is about questioning views of reality, about skills and processes firmly embedded in the child's world; it is not just a school subject with no extra-mural relevance. Writing must be a means of communicating with the child's mind, not an impediment to that communication.

References

[1] David Barlex and Clive Carré:
Visual Communication in the Science Curriculum
(Cambridge University Press 1987)

The micro: monitor and facilitator

Mary Heath

In Bedfordshire and Humberside, the focus of the teachers who became involved in the National Writing Project has been the microcomputer, and the role of word processing in the process of learning to write. The majority of the teachers were not experienced micro users themselves. Most of them had never used a micro for word processing with children, although some had other experience of word processing. They were all teachers of children between the ages of four and thirteen. They were planning to use the micro for writing stories and publishing newspapers, as well as for writing in Science and Humanities. Some of the teachers had daily access to the computer; some had access to it for a week at a time; some for half a term; one had to wait her turn in a long queue of eleven for her access to the one computer in the school.

At the computer, the children worked individually or in groups of two or three, and their writing took time. The children *wanted* to spend time writing on the micro. This motivation, involvement and concentration had to be taken into consideration. They affected the teachers' classroom management, disrupted their plans and forced them to reconsider their priorities, weighing them against the other pressures on the school day. They had to decide how much time could be devoted to word processing within the school's timetable constraints. Extra time was found before school, and during breaks and lunch-times. The teachers had to consider explicitly the options open to them and to the children, and then make choices which they could justify to themselves and to colleagues. This planning period was often the beginning of a process of reflection, a reconsideration of priorities and values which led the teachers to make changes in their practice.

The second aspect which led the participating teachers towards a changing perception about the children's learning and their role in that learning was the nature of the microcomputer itself. The open screen of the monitor enabled the children to keep the jointly composed text visible to them all. This encouraged them to read the writing aloud and to discuss it. The monitor provided an excellent focus for talking to the children about their writing and working with them *'in the midst of their competence'*.[1] For example, one boy in a group of young writers had identified a portion of a text which they all agreed should be moved. The teacher helped them move it and then stayed nearby, providing support and giving them confidence in themselves until the job was done. The writing was held steady on the screen while the group reread the text, searching and pointing at the screen as they found the words needed for the continuity of the writing. They were learning that writing is not fixed on the page; it can be moved to say more precisely what you intended. The visibility of the text on the monitor helped the children and the teachers in this.

The monitor was used by the teachers as an observation focus, enabling them to watch the children writing in a new way. They listened to them, talked to them and joined in with their discussions. (Intervention by the teacher became an important issue within the Bedfordshire project, and we are still discussing the timing and the quality of that intervention.) The teachers heard the children demonstrating their awareness of register; the reasons behind their choice of words; their concern about the appropriateness of the writing; their understanding of story structure; their ability to punctuate effectively and to spell. This close observation of what was actually happening as the children were writing, and subsequent reflection on this, extended and changed the teachers' ideas about the place of the micro and the teacher in the children's writing development. It was sometimes difficult for the teachers to tell which parts in the collaborative writing group particular children were taking. One child would act as scribe as the other child told the story, and then the first child would type as the other watched. At other times, a group would admit children who seemed to the teacher to be just watching the screen and swinging their legs. They did not seem to be actively contributing in any way, and yet those children's names were included at the end as writers, and they would gain as much pleasure as the others in reading the print-outs to everyone. The teachers had to reconsider their ideas about what constitutes collaboration to the children. They were made to think again about their expectations of, their plans for, and even their control over the children's learning. The children and the micro were teaching the teachers about children's learning.

In one classroom, three nine-year-old girls were writing at the micro. They had all found reading and writing difficult since they started school. They had used the computer for adventure games, but not for writing. One girl suggested that they write the story of Cinderella, and the others agreed. As they talked about the story they were surprised to find that they all knew the same version and that they all had the book at home. The retelling of the story was slow at first, with an emphasis on correct spelling. Gradually, the excitement of the story caught their imagination, and they reached a noisy conclusion — with all of them invited to Cinderella's wedding reception. The girls had spent the whole of a rainy morning writing. This had cut across the class teacher's plans, assembly and wet break. Because they had been given enough time, they had triumphantly produced a complete story which confirmed them as storytellers in their own eyes, in the eyes of their teacher, and in the eyes of their friends as they read the story to them at the end of the morning. They had discovered that together you can change the story you know until it becomes a new one. If we hadn't been working together around the micro, the story could not have been developed in this exciting way.

The teachers and I were particularly interested in the work we did on the micro with very young children. The screen provided a useful medium for looking at the writing together. The writing would begin with a period of experimentation and play with the letters on the keyboard and the features of the word processing program. We would watch the young child writing at full speed on the keyboard *'like a real typist'*, and then the hurried key tapping would slow down and the child would press one key with care, watching the letter appear on the screen. I remarked on this letter to Emily: *'You've written the beginning of your daddy's name! Look, "J".'* Emily responded to this with great excitement: *'I've written my daddy's name!'* Later in the term, Emily wrote a whole story for herself with the two letters *'I'* and *'J'*. She read the story to me: *'I and James went to the shops to buy me some ballet shoes for my birthday.'*

There is no doubt that the young children did have a purpose in mind as they wrote on the micro. They were playing with their knowledge about letters and choosing to present them in ways that pleased them aesthetically. Some of the children formed the letters into quite deliberate patterns on the screen, and were delighted by the print-outs. The word processor enabled the children to play with writing in this way, allowing the teacher to observe the process and talk with the child about it.

The nature of the program is extremely important if the children are to be able to write, character for character, what they have in mind. We ensured that our program featured *'WYSIWYG' ('What you see is what you get')*. Gradually, the children take over the choice of program.

We observed the children playing with ways of presenting a word. One five-year-old boy, Justin, was writing by himself, looking around the walls in his classroom to find words he could write on the micro. He turned to me to ask me how to write *'bird'*, and I told him. He then wrote, unaided, the word *'sisTer'* with a capital *'T'* in the middle of the word. He told me that it looked much better with a capital *'T'*. He deleted the *'T'* and replaced it with a lower case *'t'* to show me. He then deleted the lower case *'t'* and reinstated his capital *'T'*. This was no accidental or careless use of a capital letter. As an observer and as a teacher, I was interested in his view of writing, and glad that he had shared his thoughts about writing with me. Indeed, it may have been because I was nearby that he formulated the reasons for his decision aloud.

We would sometimes share the writing task, using the micro as a tool for writing a story or word for the less experienced writers. The child would sit beside the teacher and watch her writing. Sometimes we would type a personal narrative for a child, and this would be printed so that it could be read at home with family and friends.

Letters were usually chosen with care — meaning was always intended and could be extended by the adult — but there were times when a child needed direct help. For example, Ben wrote a group of letters which didn't seem to satisfy him. He asked me what the word said. I asked him how he wanted to read it, and he seemed puzzled by my reply. After three attempts, I asked him which word he had in his head, and he said *'chocolate'*. I wrote it for him on the micro so that he could see the word on the screen.

For the majority of the teachers in the project, the micro has become an integral, planned aspect of classroom work. The new insights about writing and learning which have stemmed from our focus on the micro have been incorporated into a workable and justifiable curriculum.

New classroom organisation reflects the changed priorities — although there is still a great deal of thinking to be done about the best way to foster and record writing development. We agreed that the following features were necessary:

- space to sit and talk

- a forum where the children could read their work to others and make decisions about the writing

- a place for relaxing and reading books, sometimes looking at them from the writer's point of view

- a place where stories, reports and poetry could be read into tape recorders

- a place where other writing tools such as felt-tip pens, pencils and paper were available, and where choices could be made about which tool was most appropriate

- a house corner, providing opportunities for play with catalogues and telephone pads

- a room where writing could be shared and followed up

Through observation of, and reflection on, the children's responses to writing on the micro, the teachers and I adjusted our ideas about what constituted 'good practice'. The micro had opened up a new way of writing and talking about writing with the children. It had enabled teachers to find out what the children knew about story-telling and to investigate their reasons for their writing decisions. The teachers could see that the micro was helping the children to talk about writing as they worked in groups; that it held their thoughts steady so that they could inspect, revise and change the text. Good writing practices were already in place in the collaborative writing groups around the micro; the open screen enabled the teachers to stand back from the teaching situation and see that this was so. This realisation was exciting and disturbing for the project participants.

The National Writing Project focus on the microcomputer has given the teachers of Bedfordshire and Humberside an enhanced understanding of the process of writing. This process is made visible on the screen. It is held up to inspection. In this way, the processes of reading, talking and collaboration which surround writing are made explicit. The next step was to translate these insights about effective learning into a practical curriculum. Thoughtful teachers, a writing project which allowed them time to work with children, and a micro with word processing program and an open monitor screen enabled this to happen.

Mary Heath — with thanks to my colleagues in Bedfordshire, and to Sylvia Emerson, the Humberside co-ordinator, for the talking and writing we did together

References

[1] Donald Graves: *Writing: Teachers and Children at Work* (Heinemann 1983)

Learning to write

Helen Henn and Georgina Herring

Most nursery and reception classrooms reflect a strong belief in child-centred, experimental learning. Children are allowed greater, or lesser, periods of time in which they can play. Play is seen as an essential element of early learning and usually involves: choosing to participate in an activity; experimenting with various materials; creating imaginative situations relating to the world they know or wish to know. The emphasis is upon children being allowed to explore and build upon what they know, and products of their efforts are displayed and valued.

Paradoxically, when teachers examine their approach to writing, these beliefs and practices are not always apparent. Children are not often provided with opportunities to experiment with what they know of print, and only perfect, adult-style writing is acceptable. This means that, in the initial stages, children's only school experience of writing may be through teacher-directed copy-writing.

A group of teachers interviewed children about their views on writing, using questions devised by Powesland[1] and starting with the request to *'write something for me'*. They created opportunities for independent writing within their classrooms, and immediately revealed how inherently useful such opportunities are. One of the significant impressions teachers have received from interviewing children is that they feel that learning to write takes place at home, not in school. In the children's responses, parents, grandparents and siblings were frequently mentioned as models. The teacher's role in writing was seen in various ways, from *'giving out words'* to *'stopping children fighting'* to *'writing it — I copy'*. This led to a reappraisal of the messages teachers were conveying about writing, and a greater value being placed upon home experiences of writing.

As parents know, young children display a sense of audience quite naturally, behaving in certain ways according to their 'public'. Children have certain purposes and outcomes in mind when choosing their behaviour for particular audiences, for in life, as in writing, purpose and audience are inextricably linked. Most adults write for an audience, be it a relative, the milkman, the bank manager or themselves. Young children are surrounded by people writing for such audiences and purposes. They bring these experiences and this knowledge into school.

As well as many experiences of print, they bring expectations which relate to their environmental and cultural background. Depending upon where they live and what they see in their immediate environment, young children may recognise and correctly interpret traffic signs, shop signs and posters. One four-year-old nursery child was able to write *'Gas'* from memory, having seen it on vans, television advertisements and posters.

Cultural experiences affect the value that children place upon certain literacy activities. Not all children will be familiar with shopping lists, while for those who have relatives in other countries, writing letters will have taken on particular significance. There is also the question of language diversity; early writing may reflect the cursive Urdu/Arabic form and be written from right to left if, for example, the home written language is Urdu:

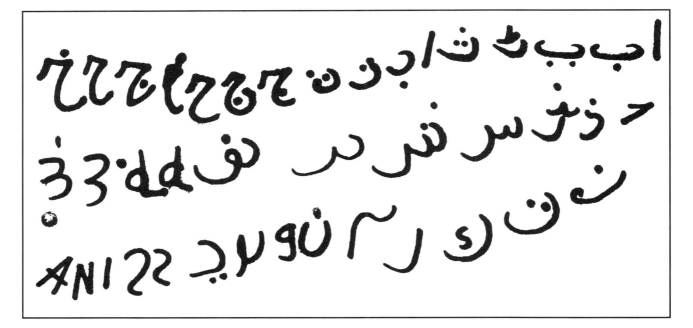

These diverse forms of written language have been used and displayed in classrooms where they have not only brought delight and security to young children, seeing their home language achieve status, but have also provided points for *'reflection on the nature and use of language'* for all children.

Children often come to school with expectations relating to gender, and these are perpetuated by the staff — albeit unintentionally. A survey carried out by Julia Hodgeon[2] on sex differentiation in the nursery identified activities in which either girls or boys predominated. Girls had a high level of involvement in writing activities, whereas large-scale construction work tended to attract the boys. This pattern was thought to be linked to the teachers' treatment of the different activities. In a school whose birthday celebrations involved all classes in examining domestic items from the 1930s, the nursery teacher found boys and girls equally keen to record their findings in writing. The subject matter for this factual writing seemed to have equal appeal to all the children. This highlights the importance of offering all writers a range of formats and stimuli from the beginning.

Important though story writing is in language development, the content is often narrow and stereotyped, girls' stories being concerned with domestic issues or *'Care Bears'*, and boys' stories with *'He-man'* or space adventures. Although we may wish to help writers to go beyond this recurring imagery, the difficulty for teachers is to assess what level of intervention is appropriate, without undermining freedom or confidence.

and on the other siud of the wold
this robot is trapt by foxman the
ledr of the foxman lifdid
up his surd and tha robot
lifdid his surds up and then a
pursn came and cild the foxman

Letter writing is an activity in which many young children are involved at home (especially at Christmas time), and when materials and encouragement are provided at school, nursery and reception children willingly write to Santa. In the following example, Katie is informing Santa that she has been good and would like certain toys in her stocking:

Children in other schools have also proved to be a popular audience for letters. When children in two middle Infant classes exchanged letters, they were concerned about all aspects of the writing. Five-year-old Esther wrote her letter (the longest piece of independent writing she had ever attempted), reread it, and underlined all the words she thought she had misspelled before consulting her teacher (right).

Dear penfriend

My name is Esther

I live in Estherf road

My mum is naughty

ror une naughty   I thef

saher is I go Togymnastics

ther goi is ror nonEaJoh

I go farm   kone·

pap lg   I'm hero

Donny her My ffo

is Donna

would like a

I'

girl

Real contexts for writing have been found in many aspects of classroom work. Role-play areas, provided in almost every nursery and reception classroom, offer major potential for exploring literacy as young children perceive it in the adult world. Within this safe environment, children are able to take on imaginative roles and to invent games.

Teachers have begun to take account of the highly literate society in which we all live, and have introduced opportunities for literate behaviour into their classrooms' home corners. Children have been given the chance to take telephone messages, read the newspapers, do the crossword, leave a note for the milkman, look up recipes, open the mail, fill in forms or write letters. The builder's office set up in one reception class gave many children new experiences of letter writing, ordering and information seeking, allowing them to learn about written language within the context of imaginative play. Many parents participated in this, writing letters to the builder. They blended reality and fantasy in their letters, just as the children were doing. This sort of role play is central to a young child's understanding of the world, and it is an important consideration when teachers are making provision for writing in the early years.

Watching adults writing can provide a powerful model. Teachers have modelled writing for a whole class, acting as scribes for group compositions or as writers in their own right, writing for or in front of the children. In these sessions, learning is achieved through interaction between teacher and child, child and teacher, child and child. Teachers have reported how keen all children are to be invited into the writing process, taking from the situation what they need to know. This might be simply recognising letters from their name; learning about spaces between words; finding out about the conventions for writing letters; noticing words within words;

becoming aware of the needs of particular audiences; seeing that mistakes are an acceptable part of the writing process; realising the importance of writing for meaning; learning that we write from left to right in English and that this is not the same for every language. This list is endless. Shared writing sessions are appropriate not only for very young writers; teachers have seen the potential for this strategy throughout their schools.

The competent writer who is modelling the process does not, of course, have to be the teacher. Many schools have forged links between older and younger children, setting aside regular times when they can meet to write and learn together, both gaining from the experience. The older pupil may learn more about the concept of audience, or simply gain confidence as a writer. For the younger child, it is a chance to see how more advanced writers approach writing, and to see the drafting process in action. Many parents, like those who wrote to the builder's office, have become involved in the writing process; under the National Writing Project umbrella, they have been encouraged to participate at home and in school. Parents have read with their children for many years; now classrooms are providing opportunities for parents to write.

As soon as young children feel free to experiment with writing and regularly produce independent pieces, it is possible to build up detailed documentation of their progress by observing them, and collecting and dating samples of their writing. Here are two examples from Matthew. His first piece of writing (right) was produced when he was four years and two months old, after nearly three months in the nursery, and the second (page 64) was almost the last piece in his nursery profile. Each example tells us a great deal about what he knows, and we can see how much he has learned during the six months between the two texts.

M   MOll7hl

MOllllOI

liIMOll

MQ ll,bl

QMOd,ll   Modn

mOHll MOiNi

MoHll

Id M ll

The writing of some six-year-olds is hardly more sophisticated than Matthew's first text, and yet they need confidence and opportunities to see themselves as beginning writers rather than unsuccessful writers. Teachers can help by analysing their texts, identifying means for development.

The classroom environment which we have described has implications for the role of the teacher, who no longer has the sole function of omnipotent director. The teacher fosters a literate environment with attractive, accessible materials, and a variety of print which is used by, and contributed by, the children. Teachers also need to ensure that this environment reflects and values linguistic and cultural diversity, motivating children to use writing for a variety of purposes. Valyn (aged four years and nine months) made this warning sign for display above the sand tray, reflecting her own use of language. (The message is *Don't mess the place up!'*)

The teacher's role is to advise and support, intervening at appropriate moments, offering constructive advice on the development of a piece of writing and responding to the content and purposes of the children's writing in a sensitive manner, however far from conventional script their writing may appear. A further dimension, which teachers may find difficult but which is infinitely useful and rewarding, is simply to observe — standing back, listening and watching as children write. In this way they can monitor children's progress and the classroom environment, and evaluate themselves in order to become more adept at helping these early writers to develop their confidence and competence.

References

[1] S. Powesland: 'Children talking about writing' from *Every Child's Language* (Open University Press 1985)

[2] J. Hodgeon: 'A woman's work' — a project report (Cleveland LEA 1984)

Writing to learn

Maisie Foster and Carole Mason

'For the writer, writing is a process, a way of seeing, of hearing what he has to say to himself, a means of discovering meaning . . .' [1]

Throughout their involvement in the Write to Learn strand of the National Writing Project, teachers in Somerset and Wiltshire have pressed for acknowledgement of the process approach to writing. The product is an important part of the process, but it comes right at the end.

Children have been encouraged to consider why they are writing and for whom. They have been given the opportunity to write for themselves through the use of reflective writing, which we called 'think writing'. Children often use a book or a journal for this kind of writing. They have total control: they choose when to write and what to write, and decide whether to share it with the teacher. Through the use of this strategy, children have been invited to reflect on their learning; to write for themselves; to create a dialogue with the teacher; to make decisions. Their writing has loosened up, and they have become more confident. A dialogue has been created between learner and teacher, helping to develop trust and new skills. Schoolchildren do a great deal of writing — more as they become older — and most of the writing is for the teacher only. Think writing is an attempt to change the focus, to give children opportunities to use writing in whatever form and for whatever purpose they choose.

Such writing does not take place in a vacuum. For children to write and learn in this way, they need to feel secure in the classroom. Teachers have developed this kind of atmosphere in many ways, working with a sensitive, accepting attitude and a commitment to working alongside the children for change and development. Didactic, directive teaching methods are avoided, and there is a recognition that the learning experience may be different for each individual, even within the same class. Value is placed on the subjective experience of the learner, and writing is recognised as a means of interpreting the world as it is perceived by the individual. The writer is given a chance to reflect, to reshape text, to fail, to share concerns.

Teachers and children use think books and journals in different ways, according to their own needs. Examples reveal, sometimes painfully, what kind of learning has taken place. Very often it is not the kind of learning the teacher is aware of, but it may be valuable for the children.

4 November.

What has happened! Has the world gone mad? I have just find out that I am in Mrs B------'s group for English. I am doomed to die in the imortal fires of Hell (or Whunwww Schools boiler room) Mr N----- can do nothing but find things wrong with me so how am I suposed to survive 2 yes 2 whole weeks with Mrs B------ I have made my will out and have asked for my Ashes to be scattered over London. (My true Home) Mrs B----- has a repu reputation to be strict. (What a under statement) I dont even know what patch I am on!

The writer is talking on to paper; the text is typically unstructured and aimed at the self as audience.

A journal is a place in which to write, freed from the constraints too often imposed by different subject areas. It is the student's voice which is important, and the teacher should respect that in his/her response. That is why the journal entry should not be marked or assessed, but simply responded to. It is a place where different forms and functions of writing can be explored without concern about spelling and punctuation.

A five-year-old is introduced to think writing by the question *What makes a bad grown-up?* She is able to write in a way which engages the emotions and the intellect:

What makes a bad grown-up
a bad grown up is a was te lih ciaran
or revun wen tay havun ben
note and the bad grown-up yn
hep the ciyod mac an tin us ut

'A bad grown-up is always telling children off even when they haven't been naughty, and the bad grown-up doesn't help the child make anything.'

A top Infant reveals what she knows about her body, and what has been important to her learning:

My Body
I think that nervesin our body Send messag
to the brain like if we toche athorn our
nerves quicley tell us to takeour hand away
Bones and skin help us not to go flopy.
Our brain helps us to think about work
and I think it helps usto move our arms
and legs. our Bones are attached
together.

Fourteen-year-old Michael gives a highly coloured
impression of his world:

> I dont feel that I have worked to my limits as I have just come from a School where we had no Freedom. It is like keeping a lion in a Zoo feeding it and looking after it and then just releasing into the wild and then expect it to kill to eat and not be killed.

Fourteen-year-old Amanda reflects on the use of
journals:

> Writing in our journals has been a bit of a drag but it's good to let a teacher read it and reply without marking it saying if it's right or wrong. It's a new idea to write down our feeling in school we've never done that before. I dont know if it has helped me but I like the idea of not being right or wrong.

Ten-year-olds were given a problem to solve, using a sheet of card, a length of sellotape, pipecleaners and a marble. The group had to keep a marble in motion for as long as possible. At the end of the session, they were asked to do some reflective writing in answer to some questions:

1 How did you solve the problem?

2 What have you learned?

3 What extra things would you have liked in order to complete the constructions?

4 What are your feelings, now that the exercise is completed?

①
We started to solve the probelom when I remeberd about a toy that cars go up and down So thats how we soved our problem at first we didnt coparte with each other,

②
I think i have learnt not to work with girls and coparate.

③ youse more sellotape moie card more pipe cleaners and lots more Time

This form of writing encouraged Jane to deliberate on the lesson, rather than simply to produce a factual record of what happened. For this class of children it was their first experience of think writing, and they used the strategy for their own individual explorations.

Journals provide a vehicle for a written dialogue between teacher and pupil. Some pupils find it difficult to approach a teacher directly; they find it easier to negotiate through writing. The problem may simply be a lack of material resources:

'This lesson we started doing something by working out who does what in our newspaper. Started writing on paper, but came to a standstill when couldn't find a book with trade lists in it.'

A supportive learning environment helps the learner to grow towards autonomy. The independent learner decides which path to follow, and yet considers other people's suggestions and offers suggestions in turn. As part of a Secondary project on World War II, thirteen-year-olds thought about their work:

'I think I am going to write a Diary and say me and my sisters get evacuated and are split up. I will write in the Diary all the letters I write home to my parents and say what it was like. In the end I might describe me going home if I have enough time. And describe what the atmosphere was like when I was reunited with my parents and my family.'

In this entry, Jan has made decisions concerning the topic and the form which the outcome might take. While her research into World War II will equip her with factual information, she is considering how to use writing as a means of interpreting that information.

If the teacher is seen as a facilitator rather than a transmitter of knowledge, it follows that the learner will be encouraged both to reflect on and to determine the learning.

In an English project, a fourteen-year-old girl suggested a way of broadening the learning. The journal has become a place for student to advise teacher, not just vice versa:

'It would be a good idea to organise trips to places of interest (with some connection to the English option) during English lessons (the Rural Life Museum for the workhouse topic, for instance).'

Secondary teachers have been using the think book strategy when asking children to make a response to literature. These literature logs give the students permission to express their feelings about their reading and to identify with characters in the stories. Pupils are also asked to reflect on their own choice of subject for a piece of writing.

'Trapped animals

I chose this theme because I strongly believe that wild animals should not be captured and shut up in cages, unless they are extremely rare and have no chance of survival in the wild.

I remember once going into a zoo and seeing a tiger just lying on the ground, staring out at people. He didn't even react when some boys poked a stick at him. His attitude stuck in my mind, sad and hopeless, martyred, as if he was saying: "Go away, and leave me alone, I have lost my freedom and my dignity, and I don't wish to be seen."

I also remember, as a young child, going into a pet shop for the first time, and coming out in tears, because of the expressions in the animals' faces.

It was remembering these two occasions that prompted me to write the following poem:'

Freedom lost _____ (2nd draft)

Furious
he rattles the chains
that bind him
to the wall

Frustrated
he lurks behind
the bars
searching for freedom

Bleeding
he wears down
his useless claws
begging to be freed

Lethargic
he stares
at the humans who cry:
Look at the tiger!

After the writing the children reflected on how and why they had redrafted their work:

'. . . changed the first and second verses around because I thought that they were in the wrong order. The verse about the tiger being furious, and rattling his chains, should come before the verse about the tiger being frustrated and lurking behind his bars, because, if you watch an animal that has been captured and put into a cage, first it is furious, and flings itself against the bars of its cage. Second, it becomes tired and frustrated, pacing its cage and searching for a way out, and it forgets its dignity, and pleads to be freed, and finally, when it realises that there is no way out it becomes resigned to its fate and lies down, and loses hope and becomes bored.'

'I changed the last line in the third verse because there were too many "freedoms" in the two middle verses.

'I did call the poem "Living death", but that seemed a little drastic, so I changed it to "Freedom lost".'

The wide and varied use of think books has been an encouraging development in the Writing Project. Teachers in the Write to Learn Project have used think books, journals and learning logs across the curriculum, in Science, Maths, PE and Art, to help children to reflect on their understanding and record their progress. The children enjoy their writing, become more committed and write with ease and fluency.

Whenever children are encouraged to think write, the teachers use similar guidelines:

- to be concerned about what the children are saying and to reply to the content
- to make it clear that spelling and handwriting are not important issues in this context
- to make it clear that the teacher wants to read what the children have to say, and to join in the communication
- to be clear about whether they want the children to use it as :
  - a vehicle for thinking/feeling
  - a vehicle for reflecting on their own learning and for sharing perceptions with the teacher
  - a record of work they have done that day, and how they wish to continue it
  - a record of how they have learned and how they felt about it
- to respect the confidentiality of the child's journal; this encourages self-confidence and trust
- to provide comments which are a written version of active listening
- to avoid a judgemental response

The potential of learning logs, think books and journals is enormous; it is, however, a long-term process.

Maisie Foster and Carole Mason with particular thanks to Barry Hulatt, Sue Budden and Garth Muton

References

[1] D. Murray: *Write to Learn*
(Holt, Rinehart & Winston 1985)

3 Looking at collaborative efforts — inside and outside the classroom

The classroom as a community of writers

John Richmond

Let us think for a moment about the characteristics of a community. A community is a group of people whose existence is defined by something more than the isolated interests of its individual members. Of course, the individual members will quite properly have interests. But the community represents a recognition of the fact that individuals have needs, too, and responsibilities. These needs will be met, and responsibilities exercised, in interaction with other members of the community. This is true whatever kind of community we are thinking of: geographical, professional, political, religious, educational. In some cases, when people speak of the 'community', the word is nothing more than a euphemism, because there is no network of needs, responsibilities and interests; there is only a collection of individuals operating independently, whose contacts with others are minimal and grudging.

Too many adults are 'walking wounded' as writers. They can write, of course, when they have to, but they do not see writing as an activity which they can approach with any confidence or expectation of reward. They make a defensive decision to write only when circumstances insist, and in their 'writing voice' there is terrible uncertainty. Beyond this large group there is another, smaller group of people who cannot write at all, in that even the barest and most functional uses of writing are beyond them.

Writing has been a matter of command and ritual. You write because you have to, because the teacher says you must. It is a daily duty. Whatever you do, whatever you learn, you end up writing about it, to prove that you were there. The writing has no purpose outside itself. *You write so the teacher can find out how good you are at it*', as one child remarked, early in the Project, when a class was asked '*Why do you write?*'

You have one attempt at each piece of writing. The routine goes something like this: the teacher asks you to do a piece of writing; you do it; you hand it in; the teacher marks it; the teacher hands it back; you pay selective attention to the marks the teacher has put on it; you put it away, or turn the page of your exercise book; the teacher asks you to do the next piece of writing.

You write by yourself. Looking up, you can see twenty-five other children also writing by themselves.

You write only for the teacher. There are plenty of people for whom you might write, including, for example, some or all of the twenty-five other writers whom you see when you look up. But only one person, always the same person, will see what you are doing.

That person is primarily concerned with the legibility and technical correctness of what you produce. Their response is sometimes bad-tempered and usually perfunctory. It ignores what you have done well, or at least done with great effort. It chides you for things which you yourself know are unsatisfactory, but offers no advice as to how to improve them.

The teacher never actually writes, in spite of being the constant source of instructions to write.

Let us now reverse this gloomy picture, pausing before we do so to reflect that many of us relatively successful writers (whether we think so or not) had an experience of learning to write which contained at least some of the characteristics listed here. The learning brain is a remarkably resilient instrument. Learner writers and readers do their best to succeed in whatever mixture of helpful and unhelpful circumstances they find themselves. We are also likely to remember the positive elements in our experience which made such a difference: the timely piece of praise, a teacher or two who did respond to our writing as if they were interested in what we had to say. Our concern is to create circumstances in which those positive elements occur normally rather than exceptionally. If we can do that, many more children will grow up to be people who can turn to writing with confidence.

In any important human activity, one of the ways in which less experienced people learn is by the example of more experienced people. If a teacher writes for or in front of children, that is a powerful message. It says that the teacher regards writing as something worth doing, something to be persisted with, something which will yield to the effort and give satisfaction to the writer and interest and pleasure to the reader. Moreover, writing produced by the teacher will be an illustration of how a particular task can be performed. We need to be careful here, and stop short of saying *'how a particular task should be performed'*. A good teacher will not say, explicitly or in effect, *'Just do it the way I do.'* Learner writers need to find their own voices, which will not be merely echoes of the teacher's voice. Nonetheless, they will find their own voices in the course of encountering other people's, and through the unconscious influences of those other voices. Among the other voices should be the teacher's.

If the teacher is a writer, (s)he is more likely to remember how acutely writers need a genuine response which attends to the whole of what has been written. Each response, written or spoken, must be part of a long-running conversation between teacher and child. The conversation can be businesslike; genuine response does not mean scattering praise like confetti. Response, though, must be offered as an outcome of involvement in a child's text, not as a summary opinion after scanning its surface.

What are the characteristics of a genuine response? First, the teacher demonstrates an understanding of what has been involved in the production of the piece of writing. The teacher knows, for example, that the act of writing shows writers what they mean. Writing is almost never the mere transcription of perfectly composed language. Those who feel a need for long stretches of composed language before they begin transcription may never actually begin. The piece of writing which the teacher sees is therefore a more or less successful attempt to deliver a body of thought in an organised way. The body of thought has itself changed and evolved in the attempt to deliver it. The teacher must show, by the nature of his/her remarks, that (s)he understands that this endeavour has taken place. Take, for example, a child who has been working on a piece of persuasive writing. Somehow, the direction of the argument is contradictory and the conclusion is at odds with the writer's apparent intention. The modification of ideas as one writes — learning through writing — is a competence which must be acquired; one cannot insure against wrong choices by drawing up detailed plans in advance. When the teacher says, *'I would say this information needs to go in earlier. What do you think?'* or *'I think we're all right up to this point, but in the next section we lose our way with all these extra details'*, (s)he is giving advice, provoking a discussion, in an area in which the child as composer has actually been.

Secondly, a genuine response continually hands back to the writer the responsibility for improving the writing, but with advice as to how to do that. We will take as an example the way in which a teacher

might draw a writer's attention to technical errors. We are not talking here about a young child whose use of conventions is inventive, transitional or incomplete. We are talking about a writer who is aware of technical errors as such, and who needs help in overcoming them. There is always pattern in error. Errors, miscues and confusions are never a random collection of evidence of ignorance or carelessness. The teacher looks for the pattern in the error. (S)he draws the writer's attention to a problem by referring to it as a pattern, and by inviting the writer to look back through the text to find examples of it. *'We've got a bit of a problem with the marking of sentences — with full stops and capital letters. There are about eight places on this page where you haven't marked the sentences. Can you find them?'* The writer will thus engage with the problem much more effectively than if the teacher had simply put in all the corrections and hoped that the writer would pay attention to them.

Thirdly, a genuine response teaches by illustration rather than by abstract principle. Learner writers overcome difficulties and grasp possibilities partly as a result of seeing how other writers have successfully managed. We have already said that the teacher will be one of those other writers; so will other children, and published authors. For example, a teacher wants to help a writer to describe a Science experiment, lay out a poem, write a letter of request, punctuate speech or make notes from a source text. In the course of the conversation it may be helpful to say, *'Have a look at how (x) has done it.'*

Fourthly, and most importantly, the responsive teacher will never forget that writers write in the hope and expectation that a reader will be affected by what they write, by the writing as a whole piece of communication. The teacher's primary reflex when reading a child's writing must be to think, *'What is this piece telling me?'* The teacher's primary reaction to the writer must be that of a person who has just been told something, and who wants to reply to the teller.

The teacher who is a writer and who knows that writers need genuine responses will also know that they need the opportunity and have the right to control and change their writing in the course of making it. Children must become critics and assessors of their own work. The writing becomes properly theirs, whereas traditionally most of the levers of control have been in someone else's hands. Handing over the levers of control, without abrogating an interest in their operation, is the teacher's job. It will not be enough, however, simply to say, *'Feel free to make changes to your writing before deciding that you have finished it.'* Initially, children will need guidance in reading and redrafting their writing — not that there are any rules about how extensively or how often children should redraft, or how they should decide when a piece is finished. It is simply that mature writers reserve the right to work on a piece of writing until they are more or less satisfied with it, and know the benefit of doing so; that right and that benefit should be available to children too.

As well as becoming critics and assessors of their own work, children can usefully comment on each other's writing. There is a double advantage to this. Most obviously, there is critical space; a writer is sometimes so close to the writing that it is difficult to keep it all in focus. Additionally, there is the gap between the learner's implicit and explicit knowledge of writing. This applies equally to all aspects of writing, from understanding the conventions of punctuation to understanding what constitutes overall coherence in a complete text. Children's appreciation as readers of writing is ahead of their active ability to structure a piece and to control its conventions. Critical reading of another's text, followed by discussion, is a way of making explicit, for a moment, knowledge which is normally implicit. What readers learn during that discussion will be fed back into their active competence as writers.

Once again, it will not be enough for the teacher simply to say to children, *'Read each other's work and comment on it however you like.'* Interactive versions of the frameworks of advice on reading and redrafting their own work should initially be available to help them to do so for each other.

However, once it has become normal in a classroom for children to read critically their own and each other's writing in progress, the frameworks of advice will no longer be needed as conscious devices. They should have become embedded in the writers' habits of conversation and thought.

The critical reader of work in progress is one kind of audience. No less important is the wider audience which reads and enjoys the product. There are numerous potential audiences for children's writing. The most immediate and available audience is all the other children in the class. Publication should be simple and frequent: regular occasions when children read their writing to the class; a folder where recently produced writing from all the children in the class can be read; extensive use of display space; book making. Beyond the class are the other classes in the school. Beyond the school are other local schools. Beyond the schools is the wider community.

All these approaches contribute to a single, central aim, which is that writing should become a purposeful activity rather than the introspective routine which it has so often been in the past. The child should see writing fulfilling the purposes which give it power and worth, becoming a better writer in the process. Purposes are social as well as individual; they involve readers (and talkers and listeners) as well as writers in the network of needs, responsibilities and interests which is the writing community.

Partners in writing

Margaret J. Meek

Children arrive in school having had a huge range and variety of language experiences at home and in their communities; experiences which will recur and evolve throughout their lives. It is outside school that children are able to work and play alongside adults in one-to-one situations; where they learn how to be a part of their own community with its particular values and taboos; where they learn attitudes which will have an effect on their views of school and their ability to make the most of school experiences.

Research instigated by the Plowden Committee suggested *'that the most vital factor in a child's home was the parents' attitude to school and all that went on there'*. This view has been supported by subsequent reports which have reiterated and developed the belief that it is vitally important for parents, and the wider community, to become knowledgeable about what goes on in our schools and why.[1]

Many parents and teachers have long felt it important to be open with one another; to see school as a natural extension of children's lives, where parents are welcomed and valued and where teachers respect the children's home experience and knowledge.

The mother of a Cleveland five-year-old spoke for many when she said, *'I wish I knew more about what goes on in the school generally and his class specifically. He usually just says "We played" or "We worked" if I ask him about his day and I don't know what's been happening all day. I'd like to go in and see for myself . . .'*

Many teachers make great efforts to build good home-school relationships — welcoming parents into their classrooms, listening to them and becoming accepted members of the local communities themselves. They believe that shared responsibility and mutual trust enable parents and teachers to work together successfully for the educational and social good of the children. Where parents are confused or doubtful about the school they may pass their worries on to their children, making it difficult for them to make the most of the opportunities offered at school. Similarly, where teachers feel criticised or ignored by parents, their task becomes more difficult.

So, teachers work to inform parents about what goes on in school and why. There are parents' evenings and open days, notices and displays, newsletters and parents' workshops. Books are lent, home-school visits organised, OU courses shared.

Valuable though these initiatives are, we must be careful not to make this information sharing a one-way process, where teachers pass on information to parents but see little need to learn more than brief family details in return. Indeed, if

we give the impression that we, the professionals, have all the answers, we may well undermine the very partnerships that we seek to foster.

Listening is important too — making time to listen to individual parents talking about their children's learning and about their role in developing their children's literacy. We can build up a clear picture of children's expectations and experiences of literacy in this way. Here are two examples of illuminating comments from parents:

'I get really het up with her, trying to teach her the letters. She can't seem to remember them. Mind — she recognised number seventy-three somewhere in town the other week — pointed it out on a shop window — and that's our house number. So she is taking something in, isn't she?'

'We talk about books a lot together — she loves going to the library. We also have quite a few word games — she's our third child so she's seen us playing Junior Scrabble etc ever since she can remember I suppose . . . I don't have any worries that she'll learn to read and write, because she's so interested in what books are about and wants to know about letters and what we're writing . . .'

There have been several studies of the literacy environment in which children grow up, showing that different cultural groups have different values, beliefs and practices concerning literacy. Thus, children's home literacy experiences are often quite different from those taken for granted by many teachers.[2] Observations such as those of Barbara Tizard and Martin Hughes[3] make it clear that children learn a great deal about language and its uses in the relaxed and interactive situation of the home. However, this knowledge is not always apparent when children enter school and find themselves part of large, complex groups, where talk between adult and child has far less give and take than at home, and where reading and writing may not be linked to any more discernible purpose than that of 'doing what the teacher says'.

Cleveland teachers involved in the National Writing Project felt that home-school partnerships in writing could reinforce the links already formed through other aspects of the curriculum, particularly through shared reading. As their thinking and practice clarified, they made comments and suggestions about the value of such writing partnerships:

- If the relationship between school and parents is good, everyone can benefit.

- Parents know their own children better than we ever can, so we need to tap into this knowledge.

- Parents want to know what is going on in schools, but are often nervous about asking.

- We have to find ways of freeing our talk of jargon, so that parents understand our explanations and are not intimidated by them.

- Working alongside other adults in school helps parents to believe in their own ability as educators.

- Some parents have unhappy memories of school — of rote learning, of failed tests, of spelling corrections written out ten times!

- Children benefit enormously from individual attention, especially if it is geared to their individual needs.

- Working together provides a shared experience for parent and child.

- Before parents can be invited to write with their children, the teacher — and the school — need to be sure of their own writing policy. Such involvement gives impetus to looking carefully at our own policies and beliefs.

- Working with a child can help parents to see the difficulties experienced by children as they struggle to express meaning in writing.

- We need parents to support what we're doing in schools. How can they do that if they don't know what we're doing?

- Parents have shown themselves to be educators at home. We need to capitalise on their ability to teach by example, endless encouragement and real interest.

- We have to think about how we are going to organise the classroom if we encourage extra adults in, so that no one feels out of place.

- Teachers may give the impression that there is only one correct way for children to learn to read and write — and that only they know what it is!

- Home-school partnership needs to begin in a small way, and develop steadily, if teachers and children are not to be overwhelmed and parents are to feel valued and welcome.

Throughout the country, teachers involved in the National Writing Project have responded to this need to make home-school partnership in writing a part of normal, continuing school practice. Many schools have found that a successful way forward is to encourage writing at home; children and parents writing together, or parents writing for their children about shared experiences or childhood memories.

Sometimes this writing may be an extension of work begun at school. It may be written in a 'special' book, kept for home-school use only. Themes — Christmas, birdwatching, a school trip — have stimulated a rush of informative and personal accounts, which everyone can share. Where

appropriate, parents are encouraged to write in their home language, sometimes producing dual text versions of their own writing or translating their children's English writing into the home language, so that it can reach a wider audience. Puzzles, jokes, recipes, illustrations and questions all appear, as families see the value of this contribution to their children's education.

A further extension of this home-school involvement in writing can be seen in a Middlesbrough Primary school, where a community noticeboard has been set up in the entrance hall. This gives opportunities for parents, staff, children and local people to write and display news items, notices about events or facilities or details of items wanted or for sale. Letter exchanges take place and a corner has been established for recipes and household tips. As parents gather in this area every day, this board has become a useful school and community facility, as well as a way of providing purposeful writing models for the children.

The teachers' response to home writing is important; written responses are time-consuming but invaluable, as families see their work appreciated and confidence grows. Sharing this writing at story time is also rewarding, giving status both to the authors and to their children! Having collected memorabilia, several schools gathered family writing together and published it in books for everyone to read and share.

Staff who have worked in this way feel that the benefits are enormous. Children want to join in and write too. They become enthusiastic about writing as their perceptions of its purposes are enhanced by seeing adult writing planned, produced, received by an audience, responded to and, perhaps, published.

Parents have become more appreciative of the difficulties of writing as well as its pleasures. They see the need for talk, before and during writing; for jotting down ideas, drafting and rethinking; for using different writing formats for different purposes. The ability to write neatly and to spell correctly in the early stages of writing has been seen to be of less importance than aspects such as planning and communication, though it is important if published versions are to be made.

An extension of this way of working has been to involve the wider community in a school project or, conversely, for the school to become involved in local issues. Family histories and autobiographies have been written, involving children in interviewing, researching and recording. More ambitiously, histories of a school or of an area have been compiled by pupils; in this work, the writing of children and of other members of a community play equally valuable parts.

As Tadley rose in status from village to town, one local school saw the need for a town guide which would be interesting for local people and visitors alike. A term's work — discussion, planning, letter writing, visiting, note-making, interviewing, researching, reporting back, selecting, editing, typing, designing, finalising — resulted in the launch, at a special ceremony, of *Tadley — a Town Guide*.

Woodcote Junior School in Croydon became heavily involved in a local campaign for a road crossing to be provided outside their building. Parents and others worked with the children to collect, select and organise relevant data; the police, lollipop ladies and local head teachers were interviewed and their views recorded; letters were exchanged with the council and with the local MP. The children needed to use a wide variety of writing formats as different purposes and audiences for their work became apparent as they went along. The particular skills of certain members of their community were valuable in helping the children to choose the most appropriate format for their purposes and then to use that format well.

Other schools have produced school or class magazines, with children, staff, parents and members of the wider community invited to contribute. This provides opportunities for writing with adults, for seeing adults write for a purpose and for reading the work of known adults, both at home and at school. Children are involved in a wide variety of writing and publishing activities — a worthwhile process, with a product that will be appreciated by a wide audience.

This need to widen the range of purposes and audiences for children's writing has prompted schools to look at different audiences within their own building and in the immediate community. Other children make an excellent captive audience, and many schools have capitalised on young children's love of stories by encouraging older children to make books for their younger friends. This gives an excellent opportunity for 'real' authors to be invited into school to share the mysteries of their trade, and for parents to be invited to help, support and collaborate with the young writers — even, perhaps, to bring along a readymade pre-school audience!

True partnerships can evolve as adult and child work together to make a book which is relevant, in content and presentation, to the audience for whom it is designed, and where the young client can offer comment and response as the writing process progresses. Sometimes, the adult role can be to encourage discussion and thought; to act as a sounding board or as a scribe; to help with drafting and editing. On other occasions, adult and child may both contribute directly to the text and illustrations of their book.

The class book corner can benefit from this collaborative effort too; the whole class makes a wonderful audience. The books — conceived, worked on and beautifully published by parent and child in the classroom — are invariably popular.

One Croydon parent summed up the feelings of many others when she wrote:

'I think it was very rewarding for both myself and the children that I helped. I didn't think myself capable of writing a book or even helping to write one, but working with these children gave me a whole new insight into school work and how it has changed.

'The children really looked forward to my visits and I must admit that I also enjoyed them. I hope that working with me helped them to realise that it wasn't "stupid" to ask for help or, on the other hand, that it wasn't always rude to disagree with an adult.

'In most cases it was like a partnership. We would discuss what was to be done and how it was to be done, but the final decisions came from the children.

'All in all, it worked out very well. Maybe having an adult other than the teacher or one's own mother to talk to about a particular subject took a lot of pressure off the pupil, and learning became fun again, as I think it should be.'

The same enthusiasm can be seen in other writing formats when parents, or older pupils, act as scribe for young children's thoughts. The children are freed from anxiety about surface features, so they can demonstrate their knowledge about language and its uses to the full. Where experiences are shared — perhaps at a school performance or an outing — adults or older children can write for themselves, alongside young children, acting as models and showing how more experienced writers work.

Of course, when parents are invited into the classroom to work with the children, they must be made welcome. Teachers must also remember that parents may feel nervous and unsure. Nor will they know where the stock is kept, or that everything stops for PE at 10.35! They need to have a clear picture of their role in helping to develop their children's writing. As teachers, we must be clear in our aims and objectives when we invite parents into the classroom, and find a quiet time to talk with visiting parents about this before they begin work.

Parents who have been involved in well thought out home-school partnerships are enthusiastic advocates of their value — both to the children and in creating strong links between the school and the home. They will talk about the work, perhaps persuading other parents to join them.

Several groups of parents whose children's schools

have been involved in the National Writing Project have met with teachers outside school hours to talk about how they can best work together to support the children's writing development. This has sometimes led to the production of attractive and valuable handouts, encouraging other parents to see how they can work with the school to help their children to become writers.

When we bring the community into schools and take the children into the community, we create opportunities and need for enthusiastic and purposeful involvement in writing. When we link this to active collaboration in writing between home and school, children are given invaluable support as they learn to write — by writing.

References

[1] R. Rogers: *Crowther to Warnock*
(Heinemann 1980)

[2] H. Goelman, H. Oberg, F. Smith (eds):
Awakening to Literacy (Heinemann 1984)

[3] B. Tizard and M. Hughes: *Young Children Learning*
(Fontana 1984)

Writing for a wider community
Margaret Wallen

Many voices during the last twenty years have urged teachers to find audiences other than themselves for their pupils' writing. The Bullock Report referred explicitly to this: *'It has long been realised, and research has confirmed the fact, that by far the largest amount of writing done in schools is explicitly or implicitly directed at the teacher . . . We welcome the development to encourage writing for audiences outside the classroom, where certain constraints and criteria offer additional challenges.'* [1]

At the time of the inception of the National Writing Project, some additional factors had begun to bring a sense of urgency to teachers' thinking about the readership for whom their pupils' writing was intended. The GCSE National Criteria for English specifically referred to *'a sense of audience'* in a list of assessment objectives. There was also a more general move towards greater accountability for schools and specific legislation giving parents the right to be involved with them. Diminishing job prospects for school leavers emphasised the importance of initiatives such as TVEI which sought to establish links between school and employment. There was a growing acknowledgement that what went on in schools had for too long been dissociated from the world outside, leading at times to a sense of irrelevance and lack of motivation in teachers and pupils alike. What was needed was a real and engaging context for classroom writing, one which was directly related to the world beyond school, so that pupils' work could take on authority and purpose. A simple idea, and one that was by no means new, offered a way in. Teachers looked around their own classrooms to find alternatives to themselves as sole audience of their pupils' work. They quickly found that children of all ages and abilities like to write for and with each other, and that motivation and enthusiasm are immediately increased when writers know that their work has a real purpose and a real audience.

Success in these first modest forays into real contexts gave the writers and their teachers the confidence to seek readers beyond their own classroom. The next step was often for another class in the same school, or a class in another school, to participate in an exchange which included writing for all sorts of purposes and in a variety of formats. Writing for other children has remained the most popular audience option throughout the country. It is probably the easiest for the teacher to arrange and manage, but for the writers, the most important factor may well be the assertion of the status of other children as audience. Children probably care far more about their peers' opinion of their writing than about the teacher's opinion.

One important spin-off of writing for children in other parts of the country has been an opportunity to learn something of the cultural diversity of present-day Britain. This is particularly useful to teachers in monoethnic areas, since it is very difficult in such settings to devise realistic activities which raise awareness while avoiding tokenism.

Closer to home, teachers have seen improvements in their relationships with their own colleagues. Infant and Junior, Primary and Secondary school teachers have been brought together when older pupils have written stories for younger. Teachers in the same pyramid who had never spoken to each other before collaborated as their pupils wrote guides to their schools for new pupils from the tier below. In some cases, writing for each other's pupils has become the major focus of cross-phase liaison and it has offered a far more productive and less threatening medium than the traditional formula of exchanging booklists and filling in record cards.

Back in the classroom, the effects of writing for a real audience were beginning to become apparent. Even the most formal of practitioners found that some things had to change once the writing became real. However, they did not see this as a threat, since the writing their pupils were producing had clearly been enhanced by the new approach, and it was left to the teachers themselves to decide how adventurous they would be in their search for new audiences.

Some of the changes were relatively small: exercise books and file paper were clearly not suitable for, say, a story for a five-year-old, and so many pupils and teachers had to develop new abilities in book making or, in the case of Secondary schools, collaborate with Art departments. Other changes were more radical, although they tended to happen gradually and so did not seem too disturbing. It soon became apparent, for example, that pair and small group work was essential if more complex written products than usual were to be produced to a deadline by a whole class. Teachers who had been apprehensive about the move from class teaching were reassured by the purposeful activity they observed all around them.

Some teachers found that their pupils would quite naturally start using each other to try out the effect of their writing while working in this way and would then go on to revise it in accordance with their partner's response. Others specifically encouraged this to happen. Either way, it was soon clear that the teacher was no longer the only person who could initiate classroom writing, respond to it or assess its success. As soon as a real reader became involved, either within or beyond the classroom, the teacher's role underwent a significant change.

Writing might now be initiated by a request from an Infant to a Junior or a Secondary pupil for a book on a particular theme, redrafted in the light of the Infant's comments and finally judged in terms of how often it was taken out of the book box in the

Infant classroom. The teacher's role had necessarily changed from controller to adviser. This shift led many teachers to make a major re-evaluation of their classroom practice, not just in writing but in other areas too, for their pupils were proving themselves capable of taking far more responsibility for their own learning than they had previously thought possible.

A significant facet of this learning has been the development of a deeper understanding of how language works, for in the shaping and reshaping of texts to fit a particular audience and purpose, these young writers were coming face to face with, and gaining control over, language in action. This experience differs radically from exercises in which pupils are robbed of the encounter with meaning that occurs in real contexts. It also sounds a warning note to those who would attempt to assess pupils' abilities on the limited evidence of decontextualised writing activities.

Some teachers now looked beyond the child audience and sought opportunities for their pupils to use writing to initiate or develop a relationship with adults other than themselves. Parents were the obvious choice, and with the younger children this was often seen as an extension of existing parental involvement in reading development. In the Middle and Secondary years, too, teachers found parents receptive and sympathetic if the context was seen to be useful and realistic, with child and adult being valued equally. This has led to some innovatory and highly successful collaborative writing projects as well as more modest but equally well received activities where parents were the target audience for publications written by children alone.

There have been unexpected but welcome spin-offs from such initiatives. Parents who had written with their own or other children began to become aware of their own development as writers and some have set up writing workshops for themselves. Toddlers who have been brought into school by parents making books for them with older children have gained a real insight into the nature of literacy. Most importantly, perhaps, teachers have realised that parents can be valued partners in developing their pupils' writing, while parents have at last been let in on the secret of what teachers get up to in class. They usually realise for the first time that both a teacher's job and the process of writing are more complex than they had imagined.

Shared experience of writing has also been a highly effective means of developing relationships with adults other than parents. The local community in general has been used as a readership for such publications as guidebooks, magazines and leaflets. Individuals have also partnered pupil writers in recording oral history, some of which has been commercially published. Where the writing has been biographical and based on the memories of a close

relative, there has typically been significant enhancement of mutual respect between the generations as well as the production of accounts which are highly successful, entertaining and often very moving. Such experiences have offered an insight into the potential of writing to validate and give order to what might otherwise have been regarded by the writers and their community as commonplace experience. Memories of older members of the community have also been used as source material for historical fiction and non-fiction, and this has involved regular meetings between the two age groups both in and out of school.

Pupils have also produced writing based on their contact with the world of work. This has proved to be a learning experience for both schools and employers, and one in which writing has helped pupils in a very direct way to deal with the unfamiliar. A welcome side-effect was that some of these pupils have passed on their new perceptions to younger children by writing books about industry. This helped to correct the impression that the world of work is confined to 'People who help us' but never get their hands dirty or, conversely, that industry is all about heavy manufacturing and nothing to do with offices, shops and services.

These projects have needed considerable planning. The most successful activities have been arranged in close consultation with colleagues and have been undertaken with the full commitment of the head teacher. Far-sighted heads have seen opportunities for the development of the school's relationships with parents, employers and the local community as well as for staff and curriculum development.

Some schools have sought maximum contact with their community by using local newspapers and radio, and there have been examples of even young children using the media very effectively for their own purposes. Benefits have been gained from this sort of public exposure: good publicity for the school, increased self-esteem for the pupils and a public demonstration of the high standards children are capable of achieving in their writing. However, the unknown general audience has not been one of the most popular. This is perhaps because, although it is the largest audience in terms of numbers and range, it allows the least possibility of individual response. Most people simply don't bother to write back, even when they have enjoyed the newspaper article or radio programme, and this is neither very encouraging to young writers nor helpful to them in focusing more clearly on their audience. Nevertheless, the realisation that they, too, have the right to use the media has been a significant one for many pupils.

The range of audiences for writing which teachers and pupils involved in the National Writing Project have found is quite remarkable, when all the variations of purpose and format are considered, and when one remembers how narrow that range was until recently. There are examples of writers and audiences in every age group and in a very wide range of curriculum areas. Writing for a wider community has challenged and enlarged pupils' and teachers' perceptions about the nature and purpose of writing, and it has extended our pupils' writing repertoires so that they are more adequately prepared for the writing demands of life in the outside world. It has been the means by which representatives of that world have been brought into contact with schools and so it has also helped to increase mutual understanding. It has enabled our pupils to develop as individuals, forming relationships by writing with their peers and with children who are younger, older, handicapped or from different cultural backgrounds, as well as with their parents and with other adults. It has thus made a major contribution to fulfilling the main aim of the National Writing Project, which was to *'develop and extend the competence and confidence of children and young adults to write for a range of purposes and a variety of audiences, in a manner that enhances their growth as individuals, their powers of self-expression, their skill as communicators and their facility as learners'.*

References

[1] DES: *A Language for Life* (HMSO 1975)

Local history in context

Chris Morris

The advantages of and reasons for providing children with opportunities to write for real (external) audiences have been well documented, but we felt that this was an area that the National Writing Project in Dudley should investigate. At the outset, we felt that the local community in the widest sense was an ever-present, readily available audience and resource for pupils' writing, and that we should endeavour to involve pupils of all ages (Infants to sixth form) in writing for, about and with this community.

In many classrooms, the teachers had always been the sole audience for all the children's writing. More importantly, the pupils were always aware that they were writing for a constant audience of one. Even when the work was eventually displayed within the classroom, the same audience of one was frequently the filtering device that sorted out which writing was to be displayed. In the Secondary sector, the advent of GCSE coursework provided an ideal opportunity to persuade unconvinced teachers that their pupils should be given a wider range of assignments involving genuine purposes for writing. Audiences for writing within the community became critical. One Secondary teacher was willing for his GCSE pupils to write storybooks for five-year-olds, but he did not really feel that it was necessary for them to read their books to the intended audience, and he believed that he himself should assess the written outcome. It was a telling exercise for the teacher and me to place the storybooks in order of merit (in our opinion) and then ask a reception class to choose their own favourites. Needless to say, the two lists did not match! For that teacher, it was convincing proof that the teacher as sole judge of children's work is an unsuitable model.

Another salutary example of pupils writing for younger children occurred early in the Project. A very traditional Middle school teacher, whose classes had in previous years spent most of their time filling class books with exercises from coursebooks and worksheets, agreed to let her children write for six-year-olds. Somewhat sceptically, she arranged frequent opportunities for them to visit the Infant school to talk with their proposed audience, and gradually became more and more enthusiastic about the process. By the time the pupils had presented their stories she was totally convinced of the value of the exercise, although she was very anxious in case parents were annoyed that the pupils' exercise books were not filled with rigorously marked exercises as before. Her fears were totally allayed, however, at the next parents' evening. For the first time, the parents arrived with real awareness of their children's work, because the children had talked about it frequently and with enthusiasm at home.

Even the most cynical teachers are likely to be inspired by the excitement of pupils who have been asked to give autographs after reading to an audience in another school. Pupils in special schools who write for younger children in mainstream schools are probably writing for the first time for an audience unaware that they are classified as having 'learning difficulties'; in their response to the writing, the audience are obviously making no special allowances for the way in which the writers have previously been categorised. The resulting increase in confidence in special school pupils has amazed their teachers, who had grown accustomed to some of the pupils refusing to show their writing to anyone. One such group of writers, having first tasted successful authorship by writing for younger children, are now producing braille and fabric books for visually handicapped children in a nearby school. There is nothing simulated about such an exercise; they are providing a valuable service for another (often neglected) sector of the community.

A noticeable factor in the success of the children's stories was that, perhaps for the first time, the children were the experts; their teachers were not in a position to tell them that they were wrong. Many Secondary school teachers openly admitted their feelings of inadequacy compared with the confidence of their pupils who had spent time talking to and reading with young children, and were now producing their own books for these children.

The writer's expertise in relation to content was another important ingredient in the success of many factual booklets. Twelve-year-old Secondary school pupils writing guides to the school for the eleven-year-old Primary school pupils due to transfer the following term were able to quell fears — about bullying, being lost in the school and many other common worries — in a way in which teachers' written guides about homework, timetables and school uniform could never do. Reception children writing guides for the rising fives — to be distributed by the home liaison teachers — were able to comment on such vital issues as size of toilets and what to do in the playground from almost the same perspective as the intended audience of pre-school children. Such language activities as these involve far more than providing more exciting or challenging opportunities for writing; they actually utilise the children's abilities for the benefit of the local community, and the end result is beneficial for both readership and school.

The sense of expertise, the confidence that a teacher will not be in a position to mark as incorrect the content of a piece of writing, is perhaps strongest in written accounts of local history based on oral evidence researched by the pupils themselves. Family history was, of course, the most accessible, but interest in the ensuing writing has not been at all parochial. When we put anthologies of local biographies on sale in newsagents' shops, they sold out almost immediately and we received many congratulatory messages. More importantly, the initial publications led to new contacts whom pupils were able to interview for specific purposes. The resulting goodwill in the community and the chance to demonstrate some of the writing activities undertaken by pupils were unexpected bonuses. However, perhaps the most gratifying message to emerge was illustrated by one pupil who was able to proclaim publicly his feelings for his father in the last two lines of his biography:

'As we approach his fiftieth birthday, we all hope he will live fifty more years.

Hugh Patrick Bell — one hell of a man.'

Many schools in Dudley are situated in multi-ethnic communities, and the public display of family histories written by the pupils benefited these communities as well as the individual writers. In one school, several pupils wrote about their parents' weddings. We were able to read about a whole variety of different customs: Muslim, Sikh, Mormon, Church of England and secular. A flood of accompanying photographs and mementoes emerged as the children's written accounts of family history allowed them to present to each other their different cultural backgrounds in a way that showed links between the cultures despite the superficial trappings. On the day that parents and other adults were invited in to see the displays, parents from very different backgrounds were able to read about each other's lives in the children's work; they ended up by talking freely to each other about their memories. Three hundred yards from the school, a wall was daubed with National Front slogans, and so we all had reason to feel grateful to the ten-year-olds who were in many ways producing a direct counterbalance to the racism which was prevalent in the community. In addition, the school was able to gain valuable background information about many of the pupils. One boy wrote:

'My mum and dad did not go to school. My mum went to the fields to take some hay and water to the goats. My dad went hunting in the woods.'

It was the first time that his teachers had had any idea that he was a member of the first generation in his family to attend school. This provided fresh insight into the attitude of his parents who did not seem at all interested in the school.

Another idea adopted by several schools in Dudley was for pupils to write a school history based on interviews with ex-pupils from various eras. Again, the benefits were twofold; language experiences and knowledge of local history for the pupils, and a chance for local people to participate in the writing process and to gain an insight into current school practice. At a time when one local newspaper was calling for a return to the teaching of grammar and proper standards in English, local people who read the paper were praising the way in which pupils had elicited information from conversations and converted this into informed and informative writing. The pupils helped many of the local people to put their own memories of school into a new perspective. When an elderly man told the pupils that school had been better in the 1920s than it was nowadays, because children had respected their teachers then, he was repeating a cliché common to people of his generation. However, when he was questioned further on this by the pupils, his answers made it quite clear to them (and to him) that by *'respect'* he really meant *'fear'* of teachers who showed no concern for the pupils' problems.

Perhaps the best example of interaction between pupils and the wider community was the writing of historical fiction set in the locality of the school. One such project involved eleven-year-old pupils writing stories set in the Victorian era. Background information was obtained via archive research, and even more directly from talking to local people who either remembered the period concerned, or were able to relate their parents' memories. The pupils made a point of posing specific questions to draw out information which would improve their own stories.

The facts that were elicited from archive research, from visits and from conversations were never required for their own sake, but were necessary to enable the writing to develop. The detailed research occurred during the early stages of the writing process, which is the reverse of what frequently happens in project work. Proof that the pupils assimilated the real meaning behind the answers to their questions is that the stories never became technical or information-saturated, but conveyed the atmosphere suggested by the research. Even if the final written product had not been of such a high standard, the process itself would have ensured that the project was worthwhile. There was, however, another important aspect. Members of the local community were involved in providing stimulus and resource material at various stages. They were involved in the classroom and, as well as being an important part of the process, were able to experience at first hand an aspect of school life which is rarely reflected in the media. The input from the community was repaid when pupils presented the fiction to various local groups — not only providing an enjoyable experience for members of that community, but also helping them to understand more of their history.

'. . . she fell and was badly injured and is frightened her family will be put in the workhouse and she doesn't want that for the workhouse is terrible these days. It's under the Stourbridge Union and there is already five hundred and seventy-four. My ma told me the jobs they do are appalling.

'On a Sunday afternoon when I take my walk I usually go past the workhouse. It's a stark place set well back off the Kingswinford Road . . . now and again ghostly white faces look aimlessly out of the barren windows and I always speed up my footsteps so as not to look for too long. It's a grim reminder of what life could be like if I were to lose my position here.'

Throughout the National Writing Project in Dudley, several conditions seem to have been important criteria for success. These include: opportunities for rewriting and editing; collaboration and an awareness that talk is a crucial part of the writing process; a sense of expertise in relation to the subject matter; growing awareness of cumulative development in the work; an awareness of the eventual readership; a sense of responsibility. These criteria could have been met in a range of language activities, but there are certain clear advantages to using the wider (yet still local) community as a focus. For example, the sense of responsibility was demonstrated in two ways. Pupils who were planning to read their stories to younger children and who had met these children on several occasions took the trouble to practise their reading amongst themselves, to try to ensure that their audience would really enjoy hearing the stories. The fact that they would (until the last moment) adjust small features of their stories to make them more suitable for the audience — even after their own teacher had assessed the stories — was a noticeable factor in several cases. Where older pupils were writing books to help younger children (for

example, school guides), they were careful to adopt a reassuring tone. While attempting to be accurate, they portrayed the information in a manner designed to alleviate worries. Their sophisticated and selective use of language demonstrated a degree of maturity and responsibility that many teachers had not anticipated. Where pupils wrote biographies of relatives, presenting their interpretations of subjects from their out-of-school experience, the benefits were obvious. The care they took in assessing whether their writing expressed what they had intended; their desire to elaborate on details in the biographies to ensure that readers would understand the significance of the events; these were noted by various observers. The pupils were assuming a direct and personal responsibility for reader response — a vital element in writing based on interaction between writers and the community.

Finally, it is worth repeating that by using the local community as a resource and an audience, we were able to benefit that community as well as the pupils themselves. The projects actively disseminated knowledge of current good practice, and reaffirmed the place of the school within the community. At a time when the ideology of market forces is threatening the idea that schools belong to the whole community, the pupils in Dudley who have involved members of the community in their own language development have suggested that, just as success in writing depends upon the context in which the activity takes place, so does the success of a school depend upon the extent to which it is part of its community.

Making links

Cath Farrow

One of the effects of the Writing Project in Hampshire has been to spotlight the fact that the learning which goes on in school is only a small part of the learning process. Children bring to school a wealth of experience, including language, and continue to build on this whether or not they are in school. Teachers have learned that if they capitalise on the learning opportunities outside school, they have a greater chance of enabling their children to learn effectively. The have found that if they continue to foster links with home and with the community outside school, this enables the children to develop into more confident, proficient writers. Inside school, they have seen that if the writing their children do is varied, has a clear purpose and has relevance to the outside world, learning is more effective. They have also discovered that by passing on the results of their investigations to other teachers, they themselves have reached a better understanding of their own views about writing and learning.

For some Hampshire teachers, the starting point with children just beginning school was the writing table. This provided a link between home and school by encouraging the children to undertake the sorts of writing activity — shopping lists, messages, letters, directions — that go on at home, as well as poems, stories or books. Even at this early stage, a sense of audience was fostered by encouraging the children to share their writing with each other, put it into books, work with a friend and send their writing to children in other classes and to people outside school.

One head teacher asked the parents of pre-school children to write to her, telling her how they felt about their children starting school. She describes how one parent responded:

'I feel sad at the thought of William going to school. I know I shall miss him. We've talked about it and he said he would miss me too, but we'll have lots of cuddles when he comes home.'

William's mum goes on to say more about her worries and hopes for her son as he starts school. Their letters have really helped us to reach a better understanding of the children. Most parents have found that they can share more on paper than they do face to face. It also establishes the fact that their writing is valued and appreciated right at the beginning of their association with the school.

This link with parents was continued by the school's three reception class teachers who invited small groups of parents into the classroom at every opportunity to see how their children were progressing with reading and writing. Home-school notebooks also gave them an opportunity of voicing their thoughts and opinions. By the end of their children's first term at school, many parents had a good initial understanding of the school's approach to literacy development.

Another way of fostering links with parents was to organise a 'Learning can be fun' evening, concentrating on writing across the curriculum. Parents wrote and illustrated 'big books', followed Science instructions, wrestled with Maths problems. Before they left, each wrote a postcard telling their child all about the activities they had done. As they worked, their faces showed the satisfaction which is seen daily in the classroom on their children's faces.

Links were also made between classes within schools, between neighbouring schools and between schools in different areas of the county. One First school joined with the neighbouring Middle school for a meeting of parents and teachers to explain their policy of shared reading and writing. To put across their ideas, they used displays and videos, and gave plenty of time for questions. The highlight was a humorous sketch performed by the staff, showing how easily parents and teachers can put children off reading and writing.

Elsewhere, older children were writing for younger ones in neighbouring schools; children aged from eight to thirteen were writing storybooks, information books and reading cards. One class of children exchanged letters with a class in another part of the county, following them up with visits which proved to be a valuable social activity as well as a real reason for writing.

A number of schools, some Secondary, fostered links with the community outside school. This was a two-way exercise, with children going out of school to meet people who lived and worked in the community and with people from outside school coming in. This proved to be beneficial for the children as they saw themselves in a wider context than simply that of the classroom. For the Secondary children involved in the Writing and the World of Work part of the Project, it gave them a taste of the future. As for the visitors, they gained a valuable insight into current practices in school.

One First school discovered that many people, from vicars to shop stewards, were willing to come into school to show the children how they use different forms of writing in their work. They were visited by a grandfather who is a published author and by visitors from Brazil who were willing to write in their own language. The children wrote letters, stories, poems and booklets, sending or delivering them to people in the community. They became increasingly aware of what the public had to offer school and what school had to offer the public.

Burnham Copse Junior School in Hampshire invited poet Gareth Owen to visit, to read some of his poems and talk to the children about being a writer. The visit caused great excitement, and inspired many of the children to write poems of their own.

'Mandy likes the mud' inspired this:

'Jonathan likes red
Zoe likes to go to bed
Vicki likes to stroke a cat
Grandad likes to wear a hat
Holly likes to eat
But Abbey likes sweets.
Jo likes to play with toys
Jodie likes to play with boys
Alex likes to mess up hair
Hayley likes her teddy bear
Mummy likes to wipe her feet
But Abbey likes sweets.'

Abbey, aged 8

An Infant school in another part of the county produced a school newspaper. The children studied newspapers, visited the local newspaper offices and decided on the news and features they were going to include. They interviewed people who worked in the school, the neighbourhood police officer and local shopkeepers. Their paper, the *Kempshott Gazette,* was professionally printed by the local newspaper and distributed around the school and the community.

Similarly, a class of Junior children produced a guide to their town. They went out of school and interviewed people who worked in the locality: vicars, librarians, doctors and dentists. When the guide was ready, they invited all the people who had contributed to the publication into school and gave it an official launch.

The aim of the Hampshire Secondary group — to forge links between school and the outside world — was achieved in a number of ways.

The team began by examining writing in school as a working tool, and extended the investigations into the world outside. They did this by looking at the writing required in the workplace, the writing which pupils have to do to reach the workplace, and some of the writing material which young people face at work.

In one school two teams of pupils, as part of their GCSE coursework, went into firms to interview a wide cross-section of the staff about their jobs in order to produce a radio programme, 'Down your industrial way'.

All the members of a fifth year English class were involved in a week's work experience. They considered many forms of writing as they investigated the working day and compared it with a day at school, interviewed people at work about their writing tasks, wrote about their expectations beforehand and reflected upon their experiences afterwards. The experiment formed the basis of a new policy which has established work experience in the school's GCSE curriculum for several subjects.

In other schools, teachers negotiated work shadowing for their pupils. As in the Primary phase, there were benefits for both parties. A wide variety of people were invited into one school, ranging from those offering fairly conventional activities, such as advice on how to write letters of application and how to conduct mock interviews, to a personnel director helping to set up a DIY self-help group on management skills for heads of department. People from industry joined in the pupils' poetry lessons and, much to their surprise, loved it!

Some teachers involved pupils in mock negotiating sessions, organised by the TGWU, which successfully illustrated the problems faced by management, unions and workforce at a time of threatened closures and job losses. Through extended role-play, pupils gained a taste of working life.

The subject of writing at work was explored by studying the induction material used by a number of major national companies; this revealed a lack of awareness on the part of employers of the need to use accessible language for young people entering employment. Another study considered women at work; this raised many issues relating to gender.

All these activities were helping children to develop their awareness of different purposes for writing, and of the different formats in which writing can be produced. The writing would not have been so successful, however, if the teachers had not at the same time addressed themselves to the problem of how they could best help the children to become proficient writers. Teachers at one First school, having discovered that their children preferred to write about home rather than about the topics chosen by their teachers, found that although the children had a great deal to say about their chosen subjects, the text was often in a random order and their writing did not always reflect the richness of their talk. One teacher describes what happened:

'We decided to help the children to plan their talk, as a prelude to their writing, by focusing on certain aspects of their theme. They might look at "What Mum looks like" or "What is special about her". This helped the children to organise their ideas and develop some of their thinking through their preliminary talk. Even so, many of the children were having problems with the mechanics of the writing and the content was suffering. What they needed was some sort of bridge between their talk and their writing. We hit on the idea of suggesting that they use pictures to plot their thoughts before writing them down. This turned out to be highly successful. From then on, it was a case of trying out a series of different formats with the class, allowing them access to a variety of approaches to the problem of organising ideas. Talk was still central to the planning.'

These techniques were later tried out successfully with older children.

Other techniques developed in Hampshire classrooms included brainstorming in order to get down on paper all the information which the writer would wish to include in the writing, organisation of these ideas by clustering as well as through pictures, note-taking, and the use of response partners. Word processors were used for making finished products and book-making skills were acquired. Children could see the point of taking time at the drafting stage when they knew how much the reader would value their final copy.

In one school, a lunch-time writing club was received with enthusiasm by a large number of children, demonstrating their commitment as writers. (They were not always the ones whom the teachers might have regarded as the most confident writers.) In another school, a corridor display inviting children to write caused a dinner lady to complain, 'How can we stop the children writing?'

None of this work was done in isolation. Teachers were continually meeting to discuss problems and to produce fresh ideas. At group meetings, held two or three times a term, they were relieved to find that others were having similar problems to theirs. One teacher described the process in this way:

'We needed time to sit down and look at our observations; to challenge our ideas and to suggest to each other ways in which the work might develop. It was through this partnership in learning both as a team of sharing professionals and as a team working alongside the children, listening and talking to them, that we were able to develop the children's writing in a positive and purposeful way. We developed our own and the children's confidence to tackle new problems.'

It soon became obvious that much of the classroom work that was being undertaken on behalf of the National Writing Project needed to be shared with other teachers in the county and outside it. Project officers and co-ordinators began urging teachers to write down their experiences in order to do this. A two-day residential course was planned for all Hampshire teachers involved in the Project, and time was set aside during the two days for teachers to write. This proved to be a crucial point in the life of the Hampshire Project. At first teachers were unsure and tentative about putting their ideas on paper, but given the time and the availability of other teachers to act as response partners they soon gained confidence. Writing enabled them to share their experiences with other teachers, and also helped them to clarify their thoughts, to develop them and to see the way ahead. Equally importantly, of course, it gave them a better understanding of how children feel when they are faced with the task of writing. Since that first course, Project teachers

have continued to turn to writing: at home, in school, in front of the children, in trains, on holiday.

These writings were published both locally, in four Hampshire newsletters, and nationally in *About Writing*. News of the Project was being disseminated, and interest was growing. There were still vast numbers of teachers to be reached, however, and to mark the end of the second year of the Project we decided that teachers were now ready to move on to another stage of dissemination, that of orally passing on their expertise. They had already had a taste of this the previous summer when they had spent a day together; they were allotted five minutes each to describe their classroom activities. This time, co-ordinators asked whether the teachers would be willing to run workshops. After some hesitation many of them agreed, some deciding to work collaboratively with a colleague. We held discussion sessions on how to run workshops and the programme was prepared. It soon became obvious that this was going to be no small event. Thirty-four workshops were planned involving forty-five people, most of whom were practising classroom teachers. During the two days of the conference, 340 teachers attended workshops, representing 134 schools.

How do you follow a remarkable success like that? We soon realised that, although we hoped that many children had benefited from the work of the Project teachers, we had not provided any activities specifically for them. If we were to stage an event in the summer of 1988, therefore, it would have to be for children as well as teachers. Indeed, we decided that it should reach as many people as possible — teachers, children, parents and members of the community outside school — for us to share our conviction that we had something to celebrate.

We decided on a series of two-day festivals, five in all, in different parts of the country. Two colleges of education and three Secondary schools agreed to host us, and invitations were sent to every school in the county. We offered workshops run by published authors, teachers, college lecturers, parents, police officers and other members of the community. The participants wrote poems, planned stories which they wrote up when they returned to school, wrote newspapers, made puppets, listened to stories and took part in drama activities. There was also a 'fairground' where children wandered at will, writing their contributions in interactive displays. They wrote letters which were sent by balloon; added to stories; tried out writing in different scripts and languages; composed poems; added graffiti to walls; wrote for Science, Maths and CDT; browsed through books; used word processors and watched videos. People from adult education, industry, trade unions, playgroups, careers offices, churches, writing clubs, local television, radio and newspapers, multicultural education, the county archives department and the School Library Service were all involved. More than eight thousand children, aged from three to sixteen, attended, accompanied by parents, teachers, governors and other interested adults. Each day there was a buzz of purposeful activity as the children looked, read and, above all, wrote. Afterwards appreciative letters arrived from teachers, saying how much they and their children had enjoyed their visit. To quote one:

'The children and staff of my school thoroughly enjoyed their day . . . so much so, in fact, that my class have set up their own mini-festival displays for the benefit of those unable to go.'

Having begun with tentative classroom investigations, the teachers in Hampshire have been able to spread their influence into other schools and into the community, growing alongside their children in confidence, underlining the strength of the philosophy of the Project: *'By teachers, for teachers, with the children in control'.*

Cath Farrow, with thanks to the other co-ordinators Ann Heslop, Roger Mulley and

Continuity in writing development

Frances Clarke

Robin Culver

The Writing Project in Rochdale was based on a pyramid of schools — one Upper school and its feeder Middle and Primary schools. Our discussions about writing were extremely useful and helped in developing shared aims and approaches to writing during all phases of education. I felt, however, that there were breaks in continuity at the transfer stages between the phases, and decided to carry out a study of children in their final year at one of the Primary schools. As the children considered the two Middle schools they could choose to attend, what difficulties did they face? Were the problems social or curriculum-based? How could they be eased? What facilities for liaison existed already? Could writing help?

Talking to the children, we found that although they were excited at the prospect of changing schools they were also apprehensive. The main concerns were about the work they would be doing, relationships with other children and teachers, and the school building. Many comments about the work were quite positive:

'I would like to do History about queens in Britain.'

'I would like to learn different languages.'

. . . but some showed more concern:

'Maths will be hard.'

'Don't want to do homework.'

Children need to be able to make links between work in the old school and work in the new. Some of them felt that when they changed schools everything would be different; the work would change completely, and they would do Maths, Science and History. They did not connect the work that they were already doing at the Primary school with the different curriculum areas in the Middle school.

Social and personal concerns were inevitable. Most common was the fear of being bullied, and other comments showed a basic feeling of insecurity:

'Can you bring toys?'

'Not sure about making friends . . .'

'I am scared I might get done and be sent to a different table.'

The children also showed concern about the physical properties of the building. They were worried about dinners and dining facilities, and about how they would find their way from one classroom to another. They wanted to know more about the teachers and how strict they were.

The teachers, meanwhile, had their own concerns about the transfer. The teachers in the Primary school felt that they knew little about the Middle schools and were therefore unable to advise the children about the daily routines and practices they were likely to encounter. They could only offer reassurance — which was not very convincing. In order to ease the transfer, they wanted to know more about the Middle schools. Teachers in the Middle schools wanted to know more about their future pupils and the schools from which they would come. At both the Middle schools, there were teachers with responsibility for liaison. They visited the Primary schools and talked with the children due for transfer and with their teachers.

In the past there has been a transfer day, allowing the Primary children to visit the Middle schools for one full day towards the end of the Summer Term to experience as much as possible of the different curriculum areas. Work begun on this day is retained by the Middle school teachers, to be completed at the beginning of the school year. The LEA record folders are also passed on at the end of term or during the school holidays. They often contain a sample of the children's writing, but this is not always accompanied by any indication of its stage of development, of how it was instigated, of the audience for whom it was intended, of the control the child had over the choice of words, or of the degree of collaboration with the teacher or fellow pupils. Compounding the problems of liaison and transfer (and making the choice for parents and pupils more difficult) are the differences between schools in the same phase of education.

When I asked the teachers at the Middle schools whether they were satisfied with their knowledge of the new intake, they all said that they were not. The teachers felt that they gained most of their information from meeting the children on the transfer day and seeing their writing. The writing in the record folder gave them some information. Discussion with the liaison teacher was the next most useful activity, although this information was second-hand. The teachers felt that they still lacked information, that it would be useful actually to visit the Primary schools, working alongside the children to discover what kinds of experience they were having in their Primary classrooms.

Through my observations and discussions with the teachers at the Middle schools, I noticed many differences in their approaches to writing. As other studies in the National Writing Project have shown, different approaches to learning and writing are often noted at the transfer from one phase of education to another. The 'Pupil pursuit' undertaken by the Avon co-ordinator, for example, highlighted how one pupil found many fundamental from the Primary to the Secondary school. A survey carried out for the Sheffield Writing Project, 'All in a week's work', showed that there was no agreement between Primary and Secondary schools on how to encourage accuracy in writing. Although a great deal of writing was done, in most subject areas it was seen as a final statement with little or no opportunity to develop the writing further. There was also great variation in teacher expectation about the use of pupils' own words, at both Primary and Secondary level.

From the children's point of view the situation becomes extremely complex. At the time of transfer they are likely to face changes in:

- school building — size and structure
- social and working partnerships and groupings
- time pressures
- home-school relationships
- degree of movement allowed
- self-esteem
- level of control

At a more specific level within the classroom, there are further differences, not only between Primary and Middle/Secondary schools, but also between schools in the same phase. These are seen in:

- the number of writing tasks expected
- the quantity of writing expected (single word/ sentence/paragraph/essay)
- the control the pupils have over the writing task in terms of choice of style and format
- the origin of the words used (pupil's own writing/writing derived from the teacher or from source material)
- the opportunities to develop a piece of writing from rough notes (expansion of ideas)
- the time available for each piece; whether it is possible to return to a piece of writing and expand on it

- the responses to the writing by teachers or pupils
- the purposes of the writing
- the consideration of appropriateness for the readership
- the expectations in different curriculum areas

In my study of some Rochdale schools, I identified the following concerns:

- The Primary school teachers wanted to prepare the children for the transfer, but had to consider differences in approach.
- The Middle school teachers wanted to know more about the learning experiences of the children before the transfer.
- The Primary school children had many worries as well as feelings of anticipation and excitement. Some had many questions to ask; some did not know enough to be able to formulate questions.

We focused on writing as a way in which both teachers and children could gain the information they needed. I found that it could become the focus of and a vehicle for liaison between schools.

The teachers were already referring to examples of the children's writing from the records and the transfer days. If they had more information about the writing — how it was initiated; for whom it was intended; the degree of control the child had over the choice of vocabulary, style and format; the level of collaboration with others — they would know even more about the child's level of development in writing.

Wanting to create a link between the schools, we decided to try a letter-writing exchange which would lead to the Primary children visiting the Middle school, with the older children acting as hosts. It proved to be a very successful exercise, reassuring us that we were on the right lines.

Continuity in writing development

— through an increase in knowledge/awareness for child/teacher before transfer

Child	*Teacher*
Increased motivation due to knowledge of the purpose and audience	Knowledge of the context of the task clarifies the level of development reached

The Primary children began the letter exchange, and it was a challenge for them to communicate clearly personal details as well as questions about the Middle schools. When the older children received the letters they had to read them critically and respond to the content, thinking back over the previous twelve months and remembering how they had felt at the transfer stage. This gave them a useful opportunity to assess their own development, and the replies they sent were generally sensitive and encouraging, written in a style appropriate for their younger audience. As letters were compared, information shared, writers identified, one of the main concerns of the younger children — the fear of not knowing anyone at the new school — was being overcome. The Primary pupils realised that they knew many of the Middle school children already — because they were either former pupils of the Primary school, or members of the same church, Brownie pack, or whatever.

When the time came for the visit to the Middle school, more barriers came down. People and places had become real and, to many, the building had become a more manageable size. The children were encouraged to reflect in writing on their discoveries, and the teachers concerned gained insights. This helped them to meet and challenge expectations, and become more aware of each other's policies and practices. Exchanging ideas, experiences and resources, they were able to move towards a shared view of writing and learning.

This is just one example of collaboration between teachers across the great divide, taking writing as a focus. Other ventures have proved to be equally successful: a joint visit to a local place of interest; a shared topic; making books, magazines, newspapers, brochures, guides and worksheets; joint research projects; joint displays of shared writing; joint events and displays — gymnastics, Art, Science, concerts; personal folders of work selected by children for their future teacher; topics spanning the transition, started in one school and continued in the next.

As a cross-curricular activity, writing provides a natural link between all teachers and children. The more teachers can meet, talk, plan and share ideas, the more they can develop a common language about children and their development. Such collaboration and the building up of common approaches to learning and writing can do much to ensure continuity in the children's development.

Write for the job

Sallyanne Greenwood

Links between schools and the world beyond provide tremendous opportunities for enriching the curriculum, and for helping pupils both to perceive the relevance of school learning, and to develop learning styles which will enable them to be adaptable and independent in later life. As the school curriculum becomes broader and more relevant, the boundaries between school and community become less distinct. Changing patterns of employment and the influence of the Youth Training Scheme mean that boundaries between education and employment are also shifting. The Writing and the World of Work project provided a valuable focus for our investigation of how language and learning could be developed.

Teachers involved in the project soon discovered the importance of sustained dialogue when talking to employers. Our attempts to discover more about the writing requirements of the workplace led, ultimately, to curriculum change. Discussions between teachers, trainers and employers have taken us beyond the superficial antagonisms that so frequently surface in isolated exchanges between people who appear to have very different priorities. What we have unearthed is a set of 'basics' more fundamental than the ones traditionally aired. Whilst doing this, and as a prerequisite for further, fruitful dialogue, we have also learned a great deal about communicating in jargon-free language. We have not created new common ground; we have simply looked harder in order to find what was already there.

So what have we discovered? It appears that both teachers and employers believe that a writing environment which enables writers to develop their proficiency contains the following features:

- explicit information on the purposes for writing and the requirements of readers

- opportunities for genuine communication through writing

- situatio⸱s where writing has an immediate effect and is ⸱art of total communication

- opportunitie⸱ for writers to negotiate and collaborate

- opportunities for writers to learn how to become critical readers of their own work and to discover that writing often has to be crafted

- a wide range of evaluation and assessment methods

Pupils involved in work experience and young employees involved in the Writing and the World of Work project have made remarkably similar observations and discoveries.

The dialogue has been productive and informed because it has developed alongside activities which have allowed employers to be involved in planning, implementing, developing and evaluating curriculum initiatives. Thus the expertise, experience and resources of non-teaching adults have been brought to bear on curriculum development and the benefits have enabled us to enrich our discussions.

One significant benefit has been that teachers and pupils, employers and employees have experienced a new situation as insiders, and this has had far more impact than isolated talks could ever have.

It is imperative that the sort of vigorous dialogue which has thrived within the Writing and the World of Work project flourishes elsewhere. At the present time, there is a danger that employers, lost in what appears to them to be a forest of acronyms, will use the old GCE/CSE touchstones in order to negotiate a path that looks familiar. They will be looking for evidence of a far narrower range of abilities than recent curriculum changes are designed to promote and accredit. There is therefore a very real need for schools to communicate their aims and objectives and explain curriculum change to employers. This can only happen if education helps industry to recognise the need for developing a completely new way of identifying what prospective employees can do.

One needs to be inside a situation in order to appreciate its complexity, constraints and possibilities. Teachers and pupils in the workplace, employers and employees in the classroom, have all gained insights that prove the value of personal experience. Collaboration has given us the opportunity to develop new approaches to standard exercises such as applying for a job, or assignments that simulate writing tasks encountered in the workplace. Teachers have observed that pupils appreciate the relevance of these only when they are placed in real contexts; they can then develop language appropriate to employment situations. Opportunities that encourage pupils to become more sensitive to audience requirements invariably help them to become more sophisticated language users. Marie Stacey, a Hampshire teacher, collaborated with a firm's personnel manager to create a real context for a standard exercise. She observed:

'The importance of a real audience now became overwhelmingly apparent. I have never seen these pupils work so hard. They had to be independent and self-reliant; I refused to proof-read any of their work. They either helped each other, or worked alone. Page after page was thrown into the bin as "not good enough". I just left them to get on with it. The sight of some of the less motivated boys, particularly, ignoring the bell and working through the whole break is etched into my memory.' [1]

When the realities of work situations are brought

into the classroom, pupils are given the chance to experience new contexts whilst remaining within a familiar and relatively safe one. Most of us face difficulties when we write in new ways or in unfamiliar situations. Dave Clarke, a Staffordshire teacher who brought an employer into the classroom to take pupils through application and interview procedures, observed that his anxious and insecure pupils actually underperformed because the situation was so realistic. This indicates the importance of allowing pupils the opportunity to make gradual connections between what is familiar and what is new.

In Project work in Hampshire, Mid Glamorgan and Staffordshire, people kept discovering for themselves that collaborative ventures result in programmes of work which have a dramatic impact on pupils' motivation and performance. Lorna Ikin, a Staffordshire teacher working with a local Enterprise Agency to give pupils a taste of creating and marketing a product (in this case a board game), has described a situation many other teachers have had the pleasure of witnessing:

'The pupils were introduced to the prototype board game and played it through. Their reactions surpassed my wildest dreams — for within a quarter of an hour they had split themselves into groups, had made makeshift copies of the game and were all assessing its virtues. Modifications, constructive criticism and extreme changes came thick and fast. They were incredibly enthusiastic — here at last they had a definite purpose to their work.' [2]

Such activities, when devised by teachers, pupils and employers together, overcome many of the limitations of commercially produced materials. It becomes possible to build in features that reflect the complexity of real work-based writing tasks, where working styles and strategies have to be negotiated and evolved to accommodate the genuine problems and unforeseen difficulties that arise. The communication is real.

Through activities, messages can be conveyed quite powerfully — not because they are articulated by a teacher, but because they are experienced by the pupils and seen to be effective by employers. The messages that have been conveyed to pupils engaged in the Writing and the World of Work project are that: writing is invariably important in people's working lives; it is a form of communication; it is a way of being effective in a job; it is a means to career enhancement. These messages are all about the power and importance of writing, and so they have a relevance beyond the context that generates them. Collectively, Project activities carry two other messages: writing, not in a vacuum but for a range of purposes, is far more pervasive in the workplace than one might imagine; because of the impact of YTS, writing is probably more important in the working lives of sixteen-year-old school leavers than it ever has been in the past.

As employers have signalled during their discussions with teachers, it is not just the more obvious things like form-filling exercises and letter and report writing that prepare young people for writing in the workplace. A broad writing diet and the way in which this is presented have far more relevance. Communicating this is, perhaps, difficult, and so it helps if pupils are given the opportunity to discover it for themselves. The types of writing to be found in the workplace are probably less varied than the types to be found in the classroom, but the purposes for writing are remarkably diverse. As one young trainee in Staffordshire explains:

'I am learning day-to-day through trial and error. The things I learned at school that are most useful now are how to take notes, how to plan and structure information . . . It would have been useful if school had recreated realistic situations such as doing several things at once under pressure. A lot of the work you do is specialised and unique to that one placement area you are working in. Obviously, technical information and vocabulary cannot be taught at school; it would be impractical and impossible, as everywhere is different. But more fundamental aspects of work — having to work under pressure, accepting responsibility and working as a true team — could be covered at school.'

This is a clear indication of how important it is to listen to young people who are able to judge new experiences in the light of old ones — pupils returning from work experience as well as employees — and is also a vindication of many projects about writing and the world of work. Such anecdotal evidence demonstrates why it is important to switch attention from narrowly defined written products to the mental processes and skills which produce them.

A number of exciting things begin to happen when pupils are using language in real situations, perceiving that their writing has a relevance beyond the classroom context. It is often difficult to create appropriate opportunities in the classroom but they can arise naturally. One consequence is that pupils' abilities, perhaps previously undemonstrated, undervalued or even devalued, can be given recognition and status. The most effective working strategies often entail collaboration. The collaboration is goal-directed, and seems to develop its own momentum. Pupils are provided with new audiences, or new relationships with old audiences, as well as fresh purposes for writing. The pupils' own experiences count; they become the experts, and so they are encouraged to take responsibility for their own learning. They have to prioritise, formulate and reformulate plans, negotiate and renegotiate outcomes, adjust to setbacks and improvise as they respond to the demands and deadlines imposed by others. As they do these things, a writing environment like the one to be found in the workplace is created.

Teachers have observed that an initial activity can often give impetus and direction to other activities involving learning through language and learning about language in use. This happens because pupils genuinely engaged in writing which they perceive to be purposeful frequently devise ways of extending the scope of projects. Teachers find it less necessary to simulate communication situations in order to allow pupils to demonstrate what they can do, or devise ways of encouraging pupils to adopt an approach to writing that entails crafting and drafting. Much of the writing generated in these situations is instrumental in achieving an outcome which does not necessarily have a written form. The writing thus becomes, quite naturally, a medium for working and learning; it is a crucial part of the process even if it is not a tangible outcome to be judged or assessed. An illustration of this is provided by a Staffordshire project in which pupils worked to produce four pages of copy for a local newspaper. The written outcomes were there for all to see, but behind the reports and articles were countless agendas, minutes, notes, action plans, journals and other aids to planning, organising and monitoring.

Teachers have also observed that as pupils encountered new experiences while fulfilling shared objectives, they tended to value each other more as resources, to appreciate the differences between people and to work as a team, assigning roles and responsibilities that individualise learning. The success of the group genuinely depends on the contribution of the individuals yet, because the environment is relatively safe, experimentation is encouraged and both success and failure can be experienced in new ways.

Invariably, the teacher who is no longer the sole judge of success or failure is compelled to adopt a supportive role and to negotiate, advise and guide during the process. Therefore, forms of assessment that are both formative and diagnostic become critically important, and opportunities to make such assessments are numerous. The traditional delayed written response to written outcomes is obviously inappropriate if the teacher is not intended to be the ultimate receiver — or indeed, the best judge — of what has been written. Moreover, teachers find that they have to learn to be more comfortable outside the transmission model; the pupils require this and curriculum initiatives encourage it. Teachers have admitted feeling superfluous as they watch pupils taking more control of their own learning. They do not feel this for long. There is a shift of attention from the products of writing and learning to the processes, and attention to the processes makes the teacher far more involved in what is actually happening in the classroom. It also provides opportunities for penetrating classroom observation. As developments in in-service training demonstrate, teachers, like pupils, benefit from experiential learning. When this takes place in the classroom and when teachers are given the opportunity to share their experiences with colleagues, they gradually identify areas of common concern.

The Writing and the World of Work projects have provided opportunities for opening up and enriching the writing curriculum. These projects also exemplify many of the features of good practice (and attendant theories of learning and language development) which have informed recent curriculum initiatives.

References

[1] The National Writing Project: *Audiences for Writing* (Nelson 1989)

[2] The National Writing Project: *Writing Partnerships (2): school, community and the workplace* (Nelson 1989)